◆◆ THE GUIDE TO ◆◆
INVESTING IN
COMMON STOCKS

HOW TO B·U·I·L·D YOUR WEALTH
BY MASTERING THE BASIC STRATEGIES

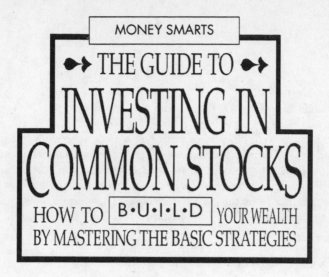

MONEY SMARTS

◆→ THE GUIDE TO ◆→

INVESTING IN COMMON STOCKS

HOW TO B·U·I·L·D YOUR WEALTH
BY MASTERING THE BASIC STRATEGIES

by David L. Scott

The Globe Pequot Press

OLD SAYBROOK, CONNECTICUT

Library of Congress Cataloging-in-Publication Data

Scott, David Logan, 1942–
    The guide to investing in common stocks / David L. Scott.—1st ed.
        p.   cm. — (Money smarts)
    "A Globe Pequot business book"—Cover.
    Includes index.
    ISBN 1-56440-142-1
    1. Stocks—United States—Handbooks, manuals, etc. 2. Invest-
ments—United States—Handbooks, manuals, etc. I. Title. II. Series:
Money smarts (Old Saybrook, Conn.)
HG4921.S39   1993
332.63'223—dc20   92-39848
                                                                   CIP

Sample stock certificate on page 4 courtesy of GenCorp, Inc.; proxy
and proxy statement notice on pages 16–17 reprinted with permission of General Motors Corporation; diagram on page 60 courtesy of
the New York Stock Exchange.

Manufactured in the United States of America
First Edition/First Printing

Contents

About the Author

David L. Scott is Professor of Accounting and Finance at Valdosta State College, Valdosta, Georgia. Professor Scott was born in Rushville, Indiana, and received degrees from Purdue University and Florida State University before earning a Ph.D. in economics from the University of Arkansas at Fayetteville.

Dr. Scott has written over a dozen books on investing including *Wall Street Words* (Houghton Mifflin) and *The Guide to Personal Budgeting* (Globe Pequot). He and his wife, Kay, are the authors of the two-volume *Guide to the National Park Areas* for the Globe Pequot Press. David and Kay spend their summers traveling around the United States and Canada in their fourth Volkswagen Camper.

Introduction

The decision to invest in common stocks is a big step after a lifetime of owning a checking account, a money market account, and certificates of deposit. The urge to shift savings from these secure investments to common stocks is generally strongest following an extended period of rising stock prices. Newspapers and television are filled with stories about the stock market reaching new highs at the same time that your friends are telling you how much money they have been making by investing in common stocks. Unfortunately, when the urge to invest is strongest, the risk of investing is often greatest.

Common stocks do indeed offer the possibility of substantially higher returns than can be earned on savings accounts and certificates of deposit. During some years common stocks provide returns of 20 to 30 percent and more, compared to returns of 6 to 7 percent that are earned by individuals who own certificates of deposit. Over long periods of time common stocks have provided substantially higher returns than most alternatives.

Although common stocks offer the possibility of earning large returns, the risks of owning these securities are real. Common stock prices go down as well as up and the prices of the stocks you own will be staring up at you from each day's financial pages. A stock may begin to decline in price soon after you purchase shares. In other words, the stock market is not a one-way road to riches. Investors, even well-informed investors, sometimes purchase stocks that decline in price. The prices of these stocks sometimes do not recover. When you invest in common stocks you must accept the fact that stocks do not offer the steady returns of some of the other investments you may have owned. Stocks offer high returns in some years and low or even negative returns in other years.

Despite the volatility of returns, investing in common stocks offers a way to accumulate a substantial nest egg. One key to successful common stock investing is to be informed about the investment characteristics of common stocks, especially the stocks you choose to own. *The Guide to Investing in Common Stocks* contains the information you need in order to make informed decisions regarding common stocks. You will learn how stocks are valued and how these securities are issued and traded. There is a chapter on how to select a brokerage firm and a broker and another chapter on where you can find information about the stock market and about specific common stocks. Last but not least, you will find a chapter that discusses the risks of investing in common stocks. It's all here in a concise and inexpensive package that is written in everyday language.

David L. Scott
Valdosta, Georgia

CHAPTER 1

What Common Stocks Represent

Common stocks represent ownership in a business. Businesses sell shares of stock in order to obtain money that can be used to acquire materials, pay employees, purchase equipment, and repay debts. Individuals and institutions invest in common stocks in order to participate in the expected profits of a business, either through dividend payments or increasing share values. Owners of common stock have a claim to the profits of a firm and generally have the right to elect the directors of a business.

Common stock is an investment that has achieved wide popularity among individuals and institutions. The public issuance and subsequent trading of shares of common stock allow you to become an owner of a business without enduring the headaches of operating the business or being held financially accountable for more than the amount of money you invest. You can become a part owner of General Motors, International Business Machines, Coca-Cola, Exxon, American Telephone & Telegraph, and many thousands of other companies that have shares of ownership that are publicly traded. If you feel particularly venturesome you may want to acquire shares of stock in small companies whose business it is to mine gold, manufacture computer components, or drill for oil. You can even purchase units of ownership in Sony, Volkswagen, and many other foreign corporations.

Evidence of business ownership is generally in the form of an engraved certificate, which many investors have their brokerage firm keep for them. An investor who purchases stock will receive a certificate imprinted with the number of shares of stock that have been purchased. If additional shares of the same stock are purchased, an additional stock certificate will be issued. If you purchase 120 shares of General Motors common stock, you will receive a single certificate for 120 shares of stock. If you later purchase an additional 80 shares of this stock, you will receive a second certificate for 80 shares. If having two certificates troubles

> If a story about the common stock of a particular company sounds too good to be true, it probably is. The more ridiculous the claims that are used to convince you to buy a common stock, the better advised you are to avoid the stock.

you (for whatever reason), you can send in the two certificates and request that a single certificate for 200 shares be issued. Stock certificates are imprinted with the name(s) of the owner(s).

What Common Stock Represents

A share of common stock is a single unit of ownership of a business. Shares of stock are issued by businesses in return for investor contributions of money or other resources. Some businesses issue relatively few shares of stock, while other businesses have sold hundreds of millions of shares of stock that are currently in investors' hands. A share of stock of a company that has only one hundred shares of outstanding stock represents greater proportionate ownership than a share of stock of a company that has several thousand outstanding shares of stock. Likewise, ownership of ten shares of stock of a company that has one hundred shares of stock outstanding represents greater proportionate ownership than one hundred shares of stock of a company that has a million shares of stock outstanding. The more pieces into which a given company's ownership is divided (i.e., the more shares of stock that are in investors' hands), the less of the whole each piece of ownership represents.

The greater the proportionate ownership of a business you have, the greater your proportionate claim to the firm's profits, and the more control you are likely to be able to exert on the firm's operations. A person who owns 200 shares of stock of a business has a claim to twice as much of the firm's profits as someone who owns one hundred shares of stock in that business. If you own one hundred shares of

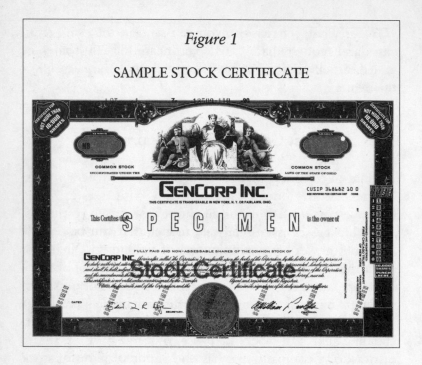

Figure 1

SAMPLE STOCK CERTIFICATE

stock in a company that has 100 million outstanding shares of stock, you have only a very tiny claim to the firm's total profits and essentially no control over the operation of the business. An investor who owns more than half of a company's outstanding stock will have effective control of the business. In practice, ownership of only 10 to 15 percent of a company's common stock will give an investor substantial influence on a company's operations.

Suppose you purchase 200 shares of stock in a company that has 200,000 shares of stock outstanding. You own 200/200,000, or .001 of all of the firm's units of ownership. Thus, you have a claim to one-tenth of 1 percent of the business's profits, and you can cast one-tenth of 1 percent of the votes that will elect the firm's directors. If you purchase an additional 200 shares of the company's stock, your claim to profits and voting power will double to two-tenths of 1 percent. Additional shares of stock must normally be purchased from other investors rather than from the company.

Why Business Issues Stock

Suppose you have an ambition to start a business but currently possess little capital (i.e., money that can be used to acquire assets or pay employees) of your own. Your first thought is to borrow the needed money, but visits to several local banks prove fruitless when the loan officers ask the amount of your personal funds that will be invested in the business. The amount of your personal investment is important because the lenders are less likely to lose money on the loan when you contribute a substantial amount of the firm's capital. Lenders have a claim that is superior to the claims of owners, which means that creditors get paid by the business before the owners get paid. Contributions of capital by owners provide lenders with a cushion that makes it more likely that the lenders will be repaid in full in the event the venture proves unsuccessful.

With little money of your own to invest, you tell the lenders that you possess great desire and knowledge, which will result in a successful business. Essentially, you try to convince the lenders that they should finance the entire operation—an unlikely event.

A potential solution to your shortage of ownership capital is to recruit other individuals who will buy into the business as owners. Rather than owning the entire business, you would then own only a portion of the firm, and the other investors would own the remainder. People will invest their own money in your firm only if they sense that it will be successful and earn a return that is commensurate with the risk of their investment. Thus, to obtain ownership funds you will have to convince other investors that your business will be successful.

Perhaps you accept the alternative of partial ownership and prove successful in locating additional investors who contribute their own funds to the business and, in turn, receive shares of stock in proportion to the amount of money each contributes. The greater the amount of money contributed by an investor, the more shares of stock the investor receives. You have chosen to give up full ownership of the business, but at least the business has been hatched.

Most businesses are financed with a combination of ownership capital (called *equity* or *stockholders equity*) and debt. The debt may originate from loans by financial institutions such as banks or insurance companies or from the sale of bonds to individual and institutional investors. Once you have successfully raised ownership capital from outside investors, you may decide to return to a financial institution and apply for a loan that will provide additional funds for your business.

Ownership capital is obtained from two sources: contributions of money by owners; and the profits a business earns and retains. An established business will sometimes produce substantial profits that provide all of the additional capital the business requires. Because a new business has no profits from prior years to rely upon, and, in fact, may suffer several years of losses before becoming profitable, mone-

---

Figure 2

PUBLIC ANNOUNCEMENT OF A STOCK SALE

This announcement is neither an offer to sell nor a solicitation of an offer to buy any of these securities. The offering is made only by the Prospectus.

New Issue

1,610,000 Shares

PAXAR
Paxar Corporation

Common Stock

Price $16.75 Per Share

Copies of the Prospectus may be obtained in any State in which this announcement is circulated from only such of the Underwriters, including the undersigned, as may lawfully offer these securities in such State.

Bear, Stearns & Co. Inc.		**Wheat First Butcher & Singer** Capital Markets
Donaldson, Lufkin & Jenrette Securities Corporation	**Lehman Brothers**	**J. P. Morgan Securities Inc.**
Oppenheimer & Co., Inc.		**PaineWebber Incorporated**
Salomon Brothers Inc		**UBS Securities Inc.**
William Blair & Company	**J. C. Bradford & Co.**	**Ladenburg, Thalmann & Co. Inc.**
Legg Mason Wood Walker Incorporated	**Needham & Company, Inc.**	**The Robinson-Humphrey Company, Inc.**
Stephens Inc.	**L. H. Alton & Company**	**Gabelli & Company, Inc.**
C L King & Associates, Inc.		**Neuberger & Berman**

May 27, 1992

---

tary contributions by the firm's owners are a very important source of funds.

Owners of a business sometimes prefer not to issue additional shares of stock that bring in new owners, who will share in profits and control of the business. If, however, the business needs outside capital in order to commence operations, or, for an established business, to grow and prosper, there may be no alternative to bringing new equity investors into the fold. If the capital contributed by new owners is put to good use, there may be more profits for everyone, including the existing owners, who will have experienced a dilution of their claim on profits and control. In other words, successful expansion may produce a much bigger pie to cut up among the increased number of owners.

The Privileges of Common Stockholders

Investors contribute ownership capital to a business in order to acquire a claim to a portion of the business's profits. The more profitable the business becomes, the more important the owners' claim to profits will be and the more valuable the ownership of the business will become. On the downside, a business that performs poorly and that consistently loses money is likely to be of little value to the firm's owners. The trick for investors is to be able to determine which businesses will be successful and which will not, and to invest only in the former. The claim of an owner to a portion of a firm's profits is the most important privilege accorded to common stockholders.

Don't put a large portion of your savings into a single common stock issue no matter how much you think you are going to make on the stock. Regardless of how sure you are that a stock will rise in price and make you a lot of money, you could be wrong.

Stockholders do not have a legal claim to a specific payment or to an explicit rate of return on their investment. That is, an investor who owns shares of common stock is not guaranteed a stated return as is an investor who purchases a bond or a certificate of deposit. The owner of a business has a claim that is subordinate to the claims of the firm's lenders. As a common stockholder you invest your money and take your chances on a business's ability to produce cash and profits. It is the uncertain rate of return that makes owning common stocks so risky.

In the event that a business is dissolved, stockholders have a claim to all of the assets that remain after the firm's bills and loans have been paid. In some instances, the owner's claim to assets is important because a business owns many valuable assets but has few financial obligations to settle. More frequently, owners' claims to assets have little or no monetary value because the business has accumulated such large debts that nothing will remain for stockholders after the debts are repaid. Stockholders of a business with $400,000 of assets and outstanding debts of $600,000 are unlikely to experience any monetary recovery in the event that the business is liquidated.

One of the rights accorded to the stockholders of most companies is to elect a firm's directors, who, in turn, establish the company's overall policy. Thus, stockholders have indirect control over a company's operations by being able to select the individuals who establish policy and who hire the firm's managers. Theoretically, if stockholders who own enough shares are unhappy with the manner in which a company is being operated, they can replace the firm's existing directors with new directors who will be more inclined to make decisions agreeable to the stockholders. Stockholders can sometimes bring about changes in company policy merely by relating their concerns to the firm's directors or managers.

Stockholders approve the selection of a firm's auditors, who verify the company's financial statements. Stockholders also have the right to submit resolutions and to approve or reject resolutions that are submitted by other stockholders. For example, an individual stockholder or group of stockholders may submit a resolution that proposes to alter the method by which elections are conducted. Or, a stockholder group may propose that the company make public certain types of information that managers have previously judged to be confidential. Stockholder approval is required to increase the number of shares of stock that the firm is authorized to issue.

Sources of Stockholder Income

As an owner of common stock you can profit from your investment in two ways: Many companies distribute a portion of their profits to stockholders in the form of dividend payments. Perhaps more important, you may experience an increase in the value of your stock during the time you own the shares. In general, if you have chosen to own stock in a company that distributes nearly all of its profits in dividends, your shares are unlikely to experience much of an increase in value. Profits that are distributed as dividends result in the business having fewer funds available to reinvest in additional assets that could have produced increased future profits. It is very difficult to find a stock that both pays large dividends and offers the potential for large increases in value. In general, growth is sacrificed for current dividends and vice versa.

Figure 3

FINANCIAL STATISTICS FOR
SELECTED CORPORATIONS, 1990

Company	Total Profit	Shares Outstanding	Profits Per Share	Dividends Per Share
Apple Computer	$475,000,000	115,000,000	$3.77	$ .45
Chrysler	68,000,000	224,800,000	.30	1.20
Coca-Cola	1,381,900,000	668,239,000	2.04	.80
Dell Computer	27,232,000	20,042,000	1.36	—
EIP Microwave	127,000	2,145,000	.06	.12
The Gap	144,500,000	151,708,000	1.02	.21
L.A. Gear	31,300,000	19,395,000	1.56	—
Otter Tail Power	24,852,000	11,455,000	1.99	1.56
Pier 1 Imports	6,600,000	35,381,000	.18	.16
Playboy	3,600,000	18,124,000	.10	—
Pulaski Furniture	5,184,000	2,842,000	1.81	.48
Showboat	1,000,000	11,354,000	.10	.10
Sony	829,300,000	372,452,000	1.85	.27
WD-40	15,490,000	7,554,000	2.05	2.02
Wendy's	38,600,000	96,000,000	.40	.24

A business that reinvests a large portion of its profits in additional inventories, equipment, and factories is likely to experience growing sales and profits in future years because more assets are available to produce these profits. When a business acquires additional assets that produce additional profits, the business as a whole should become more valuable. When the business becomes more valuable, shares of ownership in the business should increase in value. If you own the stock of a profitable firm that reinvests its income in order to become bigger and more efficient, your shares are likely to experience an increase in value.

When your investment income is in the form of dividend payments, the dividend checks can be cashed and the money will be immediately available for spending. When your income is in the form of increased value of the stock you own, the money cannot be spent until shares of the stock are sold. If you choose to own the stock of a company that reinvests all of its profits, you may occasionally need to sell some shares to have money to spend.

How Dividends Are Determined

Most companies pay quarterly dividends that follow a vote by the firm's directors. For example, an Exxon stockholder will receive dividend checks four times a year. Every three months the firm's directors meet to determine the amount of the next dividend. Depending on current and forecasted earnings, capital needs for expansion, funds that will be required to service the firm's debt, and a variety of other factors, the directors will vote to pay a certain dividend for each share of stock that is outstanding. When a company has a large number of shares of stock outstanding (Exxon currently has 1,245 million common shares outstanding), a decision to pay a dividend will require a substantial outlay of cash.

Figure 4

1991 DIVIDEND DATES AND PAYMENTS FOR K MART CORPORATION

Date that Directors Declared Dividend (Declaration date)	Jan. 22	Apr. 16	July 16	Oct. 15
Date that Investor Must Have Owned Stock to Receive Dividend (Stock of record date)	Feb. 14	May 16	Aug. 15	Nov. 14
Date that Dividend Was Paid (Payment date)	Mar. 11	June 10	Sept. 9	Dec. 9
Dividend Amount (Per share)	$ .43	$ .44	$ .44	$ .44
Total Shares Outstanding	$ 204,711,000			
Total Dividends Paid in 1991	$ 358,244,250			

During the meeting at which the amount of the dividend is determined, the directors will also establish the date on which the dividend is to be paid (the *payment date*) and the date that stockholders must be recorded on the firm's books as owners (the *record date* or *stockholder of record date*) in order to have a claim to the dividend. It is not unusual for a dividend check to be sent to shareholders a month or more following the vote of directors to pay the dividend.

Many companies have a history of paying dividends that increase gradually over time. A company may experience growing earnings, although the growth may occasionally be interrupted for several quarters or even several years. Despite the temporary downturn in earnings, the firm's directors may leave dividends unchanged or even pay a slightly higher dividend to reassure investors that the earnings decline is temporary. Sometimes a company is forced to alter a policy of gradually increasing dividends. If the business is facing particularly bleak economic conditions that directors expect to persist for some time, a decision may be made to pay a dividend that is smaller than the previous dividend, or the dividend may be omitted entirely.

The dividend decision of directors is influenced both by current economic conditions faced by the company and by the directors' view of the future. The directors' intimate knowledge of the firm, along with their insight into what the business will confront in future periods, makes the dividend decision an important piece of information that investors can use to judge the economic vitality of the firm. Some investors will view an increase in the dividend as a vote of confidence by those individuals who are in the best

Don't be suckered into some magic investing plan that someone claims will turn you into a millionaire. Any offer that promises great wealth by following some simple investment formula is worthless.

position to judge the company's future. A dividend increase that has not been anticipated by investors is likely to result in an increase in the firm's stock price.

Numerous issues must be considered when directors meet to determine the quarterly dividend that will be paid to the firm's owners. First and foremost, dividend payments to stockholders are constrained by a firm's earnings, at least in the long run. A company cannot long pay dividends that exceed earnings. A firm that earns $100,000 per year and distributes $150,000 in annual dividends is effectively being dissolved.

Dividend payments are also affected by a firm's financial needs. When a business requires substantial amounts of money for servicing its debt, paying its employees, or acquiring additional assets, the firm's directors are likely to retain most earnings rather than pay dividends and part with the earnings. On the other hand, when a firm has only a modest need for capital, the company's directors are likely to distribute a substantial proportion of earnings to stockholders. There is little need to retain a large amount of earnings when a profitable business with limited expansion plans has no difficulty meeting its financial obligations. Businesses that operate in stagnant industries tend to pay stockholders a high proportion of earnings because the businesses have little need for the money.

Voting for Directors

As owners, common stockholders generally have the right to elect a firm's directors, although a limited number of companies have issued stock that carries no voting rights.

Figure 5

PROXY

GM **GENERAL MOTORS CORPORATION**

Proxy Solicited by Board of Directors for Annual Meeting of Stockholders
Opryland Convention Complex, Nashville, Tennessee,
Friday, May 24, 1991, 9:00 A.M. Local Time

The undersigned authorizes Robert C. Stempel, Lloyd E. Reuss and Robert T. O'Connell, and each of them as the Proxy Committee, to vote the **Common Stock, Class E Common Stock and Class H Common Stock** of the undersigned upon the nominees for Director (A. L. Armstrong, T. E. Everhart, C. T. Fisher, III, M. L. Goldberger, J. W. Marriott, Jr., A. D. McLaughlin, E. T. Pratt, Jr., L. E. Reuss, R. J. Schultz, J. G. Smale, F. A. Smith, J. F. Smith, Jr., R. B. Smith, R. C. Stempel, L. H. Sullivan, D. Weatherstone, T. H. Wyman), upon the other Items shown on the reverse side, *which are described and page referenced in the Table of Contents (page i) to the Proxy Statement,* and upon all other matters which may come before the 1991 Annual Meeting of Stockholders of General Motors Corporation, or any adjournment thereof.

You are encouraged to specify your choices by marking the appropriate boxes (SEE REVERSE SIDE) but you need not mark any boxes if you wish to vote in accordance with the Board of Directors' recommendations. The Proxy Committee cannot vote your shares unless you sign and return this proxy.

PROXY

| SEE REVERSE |
| SIDE |

PROXY USED FOR SHAREHOLDER VOTING

| X | Please mark your vote with an X. | 0109 | 00005 28220 32 | 9170 | | 0109 |

The Board of Directors
Recommends a Vote "FOR" Items 1–2

This proxy will be voted "FOR" Items 1–2 if no choice is specified.

| | FOR | WITHHELD | | | FOR | AGAINST | ABSTAIN |
| 1. Election of Directors | | | 2. Ratify selection of Independent Accountants | | | | |

For, except vote withheld from the following nominee(s)

If you would like to attend the Annual Meeting in Nashville, please state the number of tickets needed (limited to immediate family) in this box

This proxy represents your holdings of Common Stock, Class E Common Stock and Class H Common Stock.

The Board of Directors
Recommends a Vote "AGAINST" Items 3–10

This proxy will be voted "AGAINST" Items 3–10 if no choice is specified.

	FOR	AGAINST	ABSTAIN
3. Stockholder proposal on compensation disclosure			
4. Stockholder proposal on pre-emptive rights			
5. Stockholder proposal on South Africa			
6. Stockholder proposal on South Africa			
7. Stockholder proposal on South Africa			
8. Stockholder proposal on discrimination			
9. Stockholder proposal on Northern Ireland			
10. Stockholder proposal on environmental matters			

SIGNATURE(S)   PLEASE MARK, SIGN, DATE AND RETURN THIS PROXY PROMPTLY USING THE ENCLOSED ENVELOPE.   DATE
NOTE: Please add your title if you are signing as Attorney, Administrator, Executor, Guardian, Trustee or in any other representative capacity.

Reprinted with permission of General Motors Corporation

Figure 6

COVER OF PROXY STATEMENT

GENERAL MOTORS

Notice of Annual Meeting
of Stockholders
and Proxy Statement

Annual Meeting
May 24, 1991
Opryland Convention Complex
2800 Opryland Drive
Nashville, Tennessee

NOTICE OF ANNUAL MEETING

GENERAL MOTORS CORPORATION
Notice of Annual Meeting

April 15, 1991

Dear Stockholder:

We are pleased to invite you to attend the annual meeting of General Motors stockholders which will be held at 9:00 a.m. local time on Friday, May 24, 1991, at the Opryland convention complex, 2800 Opryland Drive, Nashville, Tennessee.

As set forth in the attached Proxy Statement, the meeting will be held for the following purposes:

Item No. 1—to elect 17 directors;

Item No. 2—to ratify the selection of independent public accountants for the year 1991;

Items No.
3 through 10—to take action upon eight stockholder proposals;

and to act upon such other matters as may properly be brought before the meeting.

Holders of record of Common Stock, $1⅔ par value ("Common Stock"), Class E Common Stock, $0.10 par value ("Class E Common Stock") and Class H Common Stock, $0.10 par value ("Class H Common Stock") at the close of business on March 25, 1991 are entitled to vote at the meeting. It is requested that you read carefully the attached Proxy Statement for information on the matters to be considered and acted upon.

In accordance with Delaware Law, a list of General Motors common stockholders entitled to vote at the 1991 annual meeting will be available for examination at the offices of General Motors Corporation, Capitol Boulevard Building, 226 Capitol Boulevard, Suite 808, Nashville, Tennessee, 37219, for ten days prior to the meeting, between the hours of 9:00 a.m. and 5:00 p.m., and during the annual meeting.

The annual meeting is expected to conclude no later than 12:00 noon so that stockholders can take advantage of a "Ride and Drive" of GM's new vehicles and a tour of GM's Saturn Plant in neighboring Spring Hill, Tennessee. We hope you will attend the annual meeting and, if you plan to do so, please indicate on your proxy card in the space provided for that purpose the number of tickets you will need for yourself and immediate family members. Admittance card(s) in your name along with details of the day's events will be mailed to you promptly.

You are encouraged to specify your choices by marking the appropriate boxes on the enclosed proxy. However, it is not necessary to mark any boxes if you wish to vote in accordance with the Board of Directors' recommendations; merely sign, date and return the proxy in the enclosed envelope, postage for which has been provided. *The Proxy Committee cannot vote your shares unless you sign and return the enclosed proxy.*

Cordially,

Secretary

Chairman

Reprinted with permission of General Motors Corporation

Directors of a business establish guidelines for the firm's operations and select the company's managers. It is through the election of directors that a corporation's stockholders have the potential to influence how the firm is operated. Most companies conduct annual elections for directors, although individual directors may be elected to terms of several years. For example, a firm may have a total of twelve directors, with three of the twelve directors standing for election each year.

Most company charters allow stockholders one vote for each share of common stock that is owned. Thus, a stockholder who owns 1,000 shares of stock has ten times as many votes as one who owns one hundred shares of stock in the same firm. Voting for directors normally occurs at the firm's annual meeting, although as a stockholder you need not attend a firm's meeting in person in order to cast votes for the nominees for director. A company mails absentee ballots called *proxies* to the firm's stockholders prior to the annual meeting. A stockholder can use a proxy to convey his voting rights to a representative who will attend the meeting. If you receive a proxy in the mail, it will almost surely be from the company's current directors, who are soliciting your vote. In rare instances you may also receive a second proxy from a different group of stockholders, who are attempting to elect their own slate of directors.

In theory, stockholders control the direction of the firm by having the power to elect directors. In practice, individual stockholders of large corporations have little effective voice in how a company is operated. The lack of stockholder control stems partly from the fact that nominees for election as directors are selected by existing directors, who often choose individuals who are sympathetic to the views of current directors and management. Also, a firm's management maintains control of the financial resources that can be used to achieve management's objectives and to fend off unwanted proposals and nominees from stockholders.

How Shares of Ownership Are Transferred

Businesses employ outside firms called *transfer agents* to process changes in the ownership of their securities. Companies must keep track of the current owners of their securities so that the firms can send dividends, interest payments, financial statements, and proxy statements to the right individuals.

Investors who use brokerage companies to buy and sell shares of stock do not have to be concerned with having securities transferred because the task is taken care of by the brokerage company. An investor who has physical possession of securities that have been sold must deliver these securities to the brokerage firm, which will send the certificates to the transfer agent. Likewise, when an investor uses a brokerage firm to purchase securities (as most investors do), the brokerage firm will take care of having the securities registered and delivered.

Suppose you currently own common stock that you wish to transfer as a gift to a son or daughter or that you wish to sell to another investor. You transfer a security by contacting the issuer's transfer agent and requesting transfer instructions. The transfer process is relatively simple unless a registered owner or joint owner of the securities is deceased. There is no charge for transferring securities. The company whose stock you wish to transfer can also provide instructions for the transfer of its securities. Brokerage firms will take care of transferring your securities, although you may be charged a fee for the service.

How Common Stocks Compare to Other Investments

Compared to other financial investments such as savings accounts, money market accounts, certificates of deposit, and Treasury bills, common stocks offer the possibility of earning substantially higher returns although at much greater risk. The risk inherent in owning common stocks stems from the fact that returns are very volatile and difficult to forecast. During certain years, stocks produce rates of return that are double, triple, or an even greater multiple of the returns earned on certificates of deposit and Treasury securities. During other years, many stockholders actually lose money on their investments.

The volatility of returns from ownership of common stocks stems mostly from rapid changes in the stocks' market values rather than from changes in dividends. Stock prices are subject to sudden, large variations that can pro-

Don't let common stock investing consume your whole life. Many novice investors seem to find common stock investing to be some sort of drug: once they buy a few stocks and learn a little about the stock market, everything else takes a back seat. Investing is all they think about and all they want to talk about. Remember, most people are bored to death listening to your investment theories.

duce large returns and large losses, often in a relatively short period of time. A stock's price movements are difficult to forecast with accuracy. Even trained financial analysts who spend most of their working days (and sleepless nights) evaluating stocks have difficulty determining which stocks will be increasing in price and which will be decreasing.

The volatile nature of the returns from owning common stocks makes these securities relatively risky to own, especially if there is some reason to expect that you will have to sell the securities on relatively short notice. If you don't have the flexibility to ride out short and intermediate downturns in the stock market, you may be forced to sell your stock at an inappropriate time.

The volatility of returns varies greatly among the wide variety of stocks that are traded. Owning stocks in large, old-line, conservatively financed corporations is not as risky as owning the common stocks of small, young corporations in emerging industries. Careful selection of stocks is a proven way to reduce the risk you will face as a stockholder.

Who Should Own Common Stocks?

Common stocks have investment characteristics that can provide a balance to other investments you may already own or are likely to acquire. Common stocks produce returns that are different from the returns of other investments such as a home, cash-value life insurance, precious metals, money market accounts, or bonds, so that adding common stocks to an investment portfolio can reduce the risk of your overall investment position. It is generally a mistake to invest all of your money in bonds, Treasury bills, real estate, diamonds, common stocks, or any other single investment. Common stocks are appropriate investments for a portfolio that includes other types of investments.

Common stocks have the greatest attraction for investors who are primarily interested in earning income from appreciation in value as opposed to current income. In other words, individuals should generally invest in common stocks for rising stock values as opposed to dividend payments. This doesn't mean that dividends are unimportant, but the average investor in most common stocks can expect to earn substantially more from an appreciation in the value of the stocks than from dividend income.

Common stocks are most appealing to investors who have long investment horizons. An individual in her twenties or thirties will generally find common stocks a more appropriate investment than someone who is in her sixties or seventies. Most people nearing or already in retirement are more interested in receiving current income than in seeing the value of their property appreciate.

Methods of Investing in Common Stocks

You can invest in common stocks by purchasing shares of stock from a company that is issuing the shares or directly from another investor who wishes to sell shares. It is perfectly legal for you to purchase stock directly from another investor, but in practice it is virtually impossible to locate someone else who wishes to sell the stock that you are interested in buying. You will probably find it necessary to employ the services of a brokerage firm in order to acquire shares of common stock.

Many individuals acquire shares of common stock indirectly through participation in employer pension plans. If your employer offers employees a retirement plan, there is a good chance that the plan owns a combination of investments that includes common stocks. The retirement income to which you are entitled may be insulated from changing stock values (i.e., you are guaranteed a specific retirement income per year of service to the firm), but there is still a good chance that the retirement plan maintains common-stock investments that will help pay for your retirement. Your employer has an interest in the return the retirement fund earns, which is a major factor in determining the amount of money the employer must contribute to the plan.

Certain insurance contracts are actually indirect investments in common stocks. Many life insurance companies sell a retirement product called a *variable annuity* in which premium payments are invested in common stocks and payments to the annuitants are a function of stock values. Thus, individuals who purchase variable annuities have an indirect stake in common stocks.

Common stocks can also be indirectly acquired by investing in the shares of investment companies. Investment companies (a mutual fund is a type of investment company) employ professional money managers to invest your funds. You purchase shares of the investment company, and the investment company's managers pool your money along with that of other investors. This pool of money is then used to acquire common stocks or bonds, or a combination of the two securities. An individual who owns shares of an investment company indirectly owns a portion of the financial assets that are held by the company, and the value of the investment company's shares are a function of the value of

the assets owned by the investment company. Many investment companies invest only in common stocks. Some funds
even limit their selections to the stocks of companies that
operate in specific industries or companies that are located
in a particular country.

CHAPTER 2

How Common Stocks Are Valued

A share of common stock has value because of the dividends the stockholder will receive during the time the stock is owned and the price that will be received when the stock is sold. Stock values are influenced by many things, including expected inflation rates, economic forecasts, interest rates, and the general mood of investors. Many investors rely on the opinions of professional analysts to determine what a stock is worth.

As with any other asset, you want to know what a stock is worth before you buy it. Having an estimate for a stock's current value allows you to judge whether the stock sells in the market at a price that reflects its true value. A stock that is priced below its true value is a candidate for purchase. A stock that is priced above its true value should be avoided. The problem, of course, is to develop an estimate of a stock's current value that is more accurate than the value being accorded by the market.

Valuation and Efficient Financial Markets

Many economists and students of the financial markets believe that common stocks have a tendency to sell at prices that reflect the stocks' true values. If Coca-Cola common stock trades at a price of $38 per share, then $38 per share is an accurate estimate of the stock's true value. Likewise, if Vulture Mining common stock trades at a price of $1.50 per share, the stock is worth $1.50. These researchers admit that stocks may occasionally sell at prices that differ slightly from their true values, but the variations are random and generally so small that individual investors will be unable to identify particular stocks that are over- or undervalued.

The belief that stocks are priced at their true values stems from the theory that information relevant to the pricing of stocks is fully and efficiently disbursed throughout the financial markets. Many thousands of investors are constantly searching for information that is relevant to stock values. Any new information that is uncovered is immediately acted upon by individual and institutional investors, who engage in transactions that cause the prices of stocks to

Seriously consider buying mutual funds rather than individual common stocks when you begin investing. Mutual funds offer a diversified portfolio that you will be unable to duplicate. Mutual funds will also permit you to avoid the relatively large commissions that can be encountered in trading individual common stock issues.

adjust to levels that take additional factors into account. In other words, at any given time the price of a stock includes and reflects all of the information—at least all of the publicly available information—that is relevant for valuing the stock.

Not all financial analysts agree that the financial markets are efficient, at least sufficiently efficient that stocks always sell at their true values. These individuals contend that stocks often sell at prices that are either higher or lower than the prices that would be justified by the facts. Investors who do their homework and are able to uncover information that is relevant to the valuations of stocks and yet unknown to most of the investment community will be able to earn handsome returns on their investments.

Regardless of whether stocks always trade in the financial markets at prices that are justified by all of the relevant facts, there is unanimous opinion that stock values are influenced by many factors. Anything that influences a company's ability to produce current and future cash flows is relevant to the value of the company and thus affects the price at which the company's stock trades. Even if the financial markets are efficient and it is not possible to determine which stocks are good buys (i.e., stocks that are undervalued), it is still worthwhile to identify and understand how

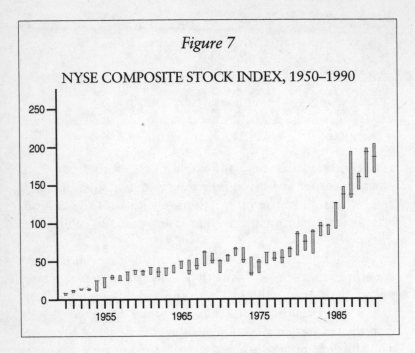

Figure 7

NYSE COMPOSITE STOCK INDEX, 1950–1990

stocks are valued and to identify the factors that have an important influence on stock prices.

Fundamentals of Valuation

All investment assets are valued in a similar manner although the process of determining the value of an asset is more difficult for certain types of assets than for others. The same fundamentals of valuation apply to rental housing, government bonds, money market accounts, shopping centers, gold bullion, and common stocks.

The value of any asset is equal to the discounted future cash flows that will accrue to the owner(s) of the asset. Cash flows from rental housing are a function of the rental income, tax effects, mortgage payments, maintenance expenses, and so forth that are associated with owning and renting the property. Cash flows from the ownership of a bond stem from semiannual interest payments and payment of the bond's principal at maturity. Cash flows to the owner of common stock are in the form of the quarterly dividend payments (if a dividend is paid by the stock's issuer) and the net amount received when the stock is sold.

The previous chapter mentioned that investors who purchase common stocks generally expect to be able to sell their shares at higher prices than they paid for them. Many—probably most—investors who buy common stocks are more concerned with increases in the stocks' market value than with dividend payments that will be received. Despite the importance that investors attach to price appreciation, dividend payments are the real key to stock valuation. The influence of dividends on valuation will be discussed later in this chapter.

The timing and size of cash flows are important determinants of an investment's value. There is a time aspect to the value of cash: namely, the sooner funds are received, the greater the current value those funds have. Suppose you have a choice of receiving $2,000 in two years or the same amount of money in three years. You would choose the earlier payment because the same amount of funds will be available to spend or invest a year earlier. You would be likely to choose the earlier payment even if the later payment were slightly larger than $2,000. For example, you would probably choose $2,000 in two years over $2,010, or even $2,020 in three years. There is some amount above $2,000 that would make you indifferent between the two payments, although the amount would not be the same for every person. The amount above $2,000 to make you indifferent is largely a function of the level of current interest rates. These rates directly influence the return you are able to earn.

The value of an asset is also influenced by the certainty of the investment's expected cash flows. Certainty refers to the likelihood that the cash flows will occur as forecast. The more certain an expected cash flow, the greater the present value of the cash flow. Suppose you have the choice of two investments. A certificate of deposit returns $10,000 in five years. You have no doubts that the payment will occur as promised because it is guaranteed by a government agency. An alternative investment offers the same expected payment of $10,000, but the actual payment to be received from this second investment could range anywhere from $5,000 to $15,000. Even though this second investment has the same *expected* payment as the certificate of deposit, the uncertainty of *exactly* how much money the alternative investment will return detracts from its value such that the majority of investors will choose to invest in the certificate of deposit.

To summarize, an investment is valued for the cash flows that are expected to accrue from it to the owner of the investment. The larger the cash flows, the sooner they occur, and the more certain they are to take place, the more valuable the investment.

Valuing Business

Because a share of common stock is a piece of ownership in a business, the value of the share of stock depends on the value of the business. A business that is awarded a big government contract or that announces the development of an important new product will be viewed as having increased value (the business's future cash flows should now be larger than previously expected), and there will be an increase in the price of the company's stock. On the other hand, if a business reports unexpectedly poor profits or announces the resignation of several important executives, the business will have a reduced value, and the price of the firm's common stock will decline. The price of a company's stock is a representation of the value of the company.

Like any investment, a business is valued for the cash flows that the business is expected to produce. The larger the amounts of the cash flows, the sooner they will occur, and the greater the certainty that they will occur as expected, the more valuable the business. A business normally produces cash flows on an ongoing basis by selling products or services to its customers. The costs of producing and selling these goods or services are deducted from the cash that is received from sales. Production and selling costs include materials, salaries, wages, equipment acquisition, and upkeep. Most businesses will also have to pay interest expenses on borrowed money and a variety of taxes. The owners (common stockholders) of a business have a claim to the cash flows that remain after all of these other individuals, organizations, and governments have been paid.

> Many mutual funds do not charge a sales or redemption fee, thus saving you substantial amounts of money. There is no evidence that mutual funds with sales or redemption fees provide better returns than mutual funds without these fees. Inquire about sales or redemption fees before you commit money to a mutual fund.

The value of business ownership is a function of the cash flows the business is *expected* to produce for the owners. Expectations change, of course, and the value of any business is in a constant state of flux. Interest rates, inflationary expectations, business conditions, and political concerns are a few of the many considerations that affect a firm's expected cash flows. Any changes that result in the expectation of reduced cash flows will tend to lower the current value of a business, as will any events that cause concern over the certainty of the cash flows to be produced. You can view a business as a cash machine. Anything that increases the size, speeds up the timing, or increases the certainty of the cash flows will make the cash machine more valuable. The same factors will influence the value of shares of common stock that you own.

The Importance of the Number of Ownership Shares

Shares of common stock are units of ownership in a business, and the value of the shares is a measure of the value of the business. The greater the number of units of ownership (shares of stock) of a given business that are outstanding, the less each unit of ownership is worth. Suppose that a business, Rushville Rockola Drive-In, is currently valued at $1,000,000. If the firm had 100,000 shares of common stock in the hands of owners, each share of stock would have a value of $10. If Rushville Rockola had only 50,000 shares of ownership outstanding, the shares would each be valued at $20. The more pieces into which a pie is cut, the smaller the size of each piece.

Dividend reinvestment plans offer an inexpensive method of acquiring more shares of a company in which you already own stock. Dividend reinvestment plans involve the automatic reinvestment of your dividends in more shares of common stock. Most companies pick up the cost of the plan and the commissions to buy new shares.

The inverse relationship between the number of shares of ownership and the value of each share of ownership may seem self-evident, but novice investors often want to know why the stock of a particular company sells at a lower price than the stock of a smaller competing company with substantially fewer revenues and profits. The answer is likely to be that the larger company has many more shares of ownership outstanding. Even though the bigger company may have a greater total value then the smaller company, the larger number of ownership shares may make each of the shares sell at a relatively low price.

An increase in a firm's outstanding shares of stock that is not accompanied by a corresponding increase in assets or earnings will cause a decrease in the value of each share. For example, if a firm's directors vote to double the number of shares of a company's stock (this is called a *two-for-one stock split*), there is every reason to expect that the value of each share will be reduced by half. On the other hand, if the directors decide to sell additional shares of stock in order to raise additional funds, the value of a share of stock may not decline at all. When new stock is sold to investors, the company ends up with additional assets and earnings power that can offset the additional shares of ownership because the total value of the company is greater than before the new stock was sold.

The Importance of Expected Dividends

Dividends are the portion of a firm's earnings that are paid to the owners of a business. The greater the amount of dividends a business is expected to pay, the sooner those dividends are expected to be paid, and the more certain the investment community is that the dividends will occur as expected, the greater the value of the business.

The proportion of earnings that will be paid in dividends is determined by the firm's directors. Dividends are constrained by earnings although directors will occasionally decide to pay dividends that are greater than the firm's current earnings. The directors' decision as to the proportion of earnings to pay in dividends and the proportion to reinvest in additional assets has an impact on the value of the business and the firm's stock.

The greater the proportion of earnings that directors decide to reinvest, the higher future earnings of the firm should be. This relationship assumes that reinvested funds are used to acquire profitable assets. These higher future earnings, in turn, provide a larger base from which to pay future dividends. In a way, a decision to reinvest current earnings is also a decision that will enable the firm to pay relatively large dividends in future periods. Thus, stocks that pay no current dividends have value because of investors' expectations regarding future dividends.

What if you purchase shares of stock on the basis of dividends that are expected during the next several years plus an anticipated price at which the stock will be sold? The truth is that at the time you intend to sell the stock, its value will be a function of expected dividends from that point on. Suppose you purchase one hundred shares of a stock that currently sells for $45.00. The stock is currently paying a dividend of $2.50, and you expect to receive dividends during the next two years of $2.70 and $3.00, at which time you expect to be able to sell the stock for $55.00. Your judgment of the stock's current value is a function of three future cash flows: two dividend payments and the expected proceeds from selling the stock. The actual price at which you sell your shares will be determined by other investors' dividend expectations at the time your shares are sold. In other words, the future price for a stock always translates into the present value of the firm's future dividend payments at the time the price is calculated. Stock values cannot be isolated from dividend expectations.

Because dividends are so important in determining stock values, investors' expectations regarding whether a firm's dividends will increase, remain constant, or decrease have a major impact on a stock's market value. Common stocks of firms paying dividends that are expected to increase in future years command relatively high prices relative to current earnings and current dividends. The more rapidly dividends are expected to grow, the higher the price at which the stock will sell. At the opposite end of the spectrum, common stocks of companies with dividends that are expected to decrease command relatively low prices relative to current earnings and current dividends. Common stocks paying dividends that are expected to remain constant have stock values relative to dividend payments that are somewhere between the relative values of the other two groups of stocks.

Because the expected growth rate of dividends has such a strong influence on a stock's value, a change in expectations regarding a stock's growth rate will have a major impact on its market price. Suppose a stock sells at a price that assumes dividends will grow by 15 percent annually throughout the foreseeable future. Now suppose there is some unexpected event, such as a report that the firm's product causes cancer or a political revolution in a foreign country where the company conducts much of its business. If the event causes investors to reassess the company's future and reevaluate downward the expected growth rate in dividends, the stock price is likely to decline, perhaps substantially. On the other hand, if a company announces favorable news that takes the investment community by surprise—a major oil find, favorable tests of a new medication, successful development of an advanced microchip—investors are likely to revise upward their expectations regarding dividend growth, thereby placing a higher value on the firm's stock.

How Stock Values Are Influenced by Interest Rates

Interest rates have a powerful effect on stock values. Rising interest rates exert a downward pressure on stock prices, while falling interest rates tend to move stock prices upward. The greater the movement in interest rates, the greater the movement in stock prices. There are several ways in which interest rates can affect common-stock prices.

Most companies finance assets and a portion of their operations with a combination of money that is borrowed

Continually review your investment portfolio with an eye toward eliminating stocks that no longer fit your goals. A common stock that met your needs several years ago may not meet them any longer.

from lenders and equity that is supplied by owners. Interest that must be paid to lenders on the borrowed funds is a cost of doing business that can have a substantial effect on profits earned by the firm and dividends paid to stockholders. When market rates of interest fall, the firm's interest expense will decline, thereby producing higher profits and a larger earnings base for future dividends. An increase in interest rates will increase the interest expense of most firms, thereby reducing profits and making it more difficult for a firm's directors to raise dividends to stockholders. Some firms operate without using much borrowed money. The profits of these firms will remain relatively unaffected by changes in interest rates.

Changes in interest rates have a greater effect on the profits of some firms than of others. For example, companies often borrow money for long periods of time at fixed rates of interest. Changes in interest rates do not affect the cost of existing long-term loans because interest on a loan is specified at the time the funds are borrowed. Changes in interest rates *do* affect the cost of money that is borrowed subsequent to an increase or decrease in interest.

Companies often borrow considerable amounts of money on a short-term basis. Companies generally use short-term loans to pay for inventory and to finance credit sales to customers. Interest rates on short-term loans usually stipulate a variable interest rate that changes automatically when market rates of interest change. Changes in the interest rate a company is charged on loans will result in changes in the firm's interest expenses. Companies that have large amounts of short-term debt will experience particularly large changes in income when there are major changes in interest rates.

Interest rates have another, even more important, influence on common-stock prices. Interest rates are an indication of the returns you can earn by owning alternative investments such as money market accounts, treasury securities, and corporate bonds. In other words, interest rates represent the opportunity cost of an investor's funds. The greater the opportunity cost of investing in common stocks (i.e., the higher the returns that can be earned on alternative investments), the higher the rate of return you will demand from stocks. To put it differently, the more interest rates climb, the higher the rate of return common stocks must be expected to provide in order to attract investors' funds. For an expected stream of future dividends, a common stock can only provide a higher expected return by selling at a lower price.

When interest rates are falling, common stocks do not have to provide as high an expected rate of return in order to attract investors' money. Investors will accept a lower expected return from stocks when corporate bonds are providing a 7 percent annual return than they will when corporate bonds are paying a 10 percent annual return. Falling interest rates have the effect of increasing the value (stock price) of a given stream of income (dividends). Rising interest rates have the opposite effect of making a given stream of income less valuable.

How Stock Values
Are Influenced by Inflation

At any given time, an investment is valued on the basis of certain assumptions regarding economic activity, inflation, interest rates, political stability, and so forth. Thus, a stock's

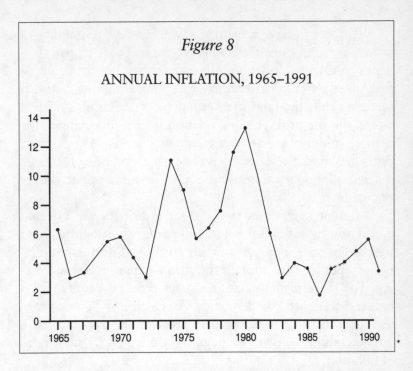

Figure 8

ANNUAL INFLATION, 1965–1991

current market price always incorporates a consensus expectation relative to many factors, including future inflation. If increased inflation is currently anticipated by the financial community, then higher future inflation rates are already incorporated into the value that investors perceive for a stock, and, thus, the price at which the stock trades. Investors' expectations may be wrong, of course, and members of the financial community are continually altering their assessments of the variables that affect stock values. The important thing to understand is that factors other than current inflation and current changes in inflation are important in valuing stocks. Changes in *expectations* regarding inflation also have the power to move stock prices.

Inflation can have a major impact on the profitability of a business and, thus, the ability of the business to pay dividends to owners. Inflation influences the prices that companies must pay for materials, labor, and equipment, and it increases the cost (and market value) of buildings and real estate. On the positive side, inflation is likely to increase the market values of many of a company's assets. Also, certain firms may find it relatively easy to pass along price increases during inflationary times without suffering a public outcry or customer backlash.

Different companies in different industries are affected differently by inflation. Some companies find it difficult to pass along price increases to their customers during an inflationary period even though the firms' expenses are increasing. For these firms, inflation causes reduced profits and a reduced ability to pay dividends. An electric utility that cannot raise its rates until the firm receives the approval of a public commission will be negatively affected by high rates of inflation.

Some companies are able to sell their products or services at substantially higher prices even though the companies have relatively stable costs. Inflation proves beneficial to these companies, which are able to earn higher profits and have the resources to pay increased dividends. Mining companies, for example, often have a large amount of fixed expenses and are able to sell their products at substantially higher prices during inflationary periods. These firms should benefit from an inflationary environment.

Inflationary expectations influence the rate at which investors discount future dividends. Inflation affects the rate of discount by influencing interest rates. When the financial markets anticipate rising inflation, interest rates increase as lenders demand higher rates to offset their expectation of having loans repaid in less valuable dollars. Conversely, when inflationary expectations decline, interest rates will also generally decline. As discussed earlier in this chapter, rising interest rates have a negative influence on stock prices, while falling interest rates have a positive influence on common-stock values. Because expected inflation has an influence on interest rates, expected inflation also has an impact on common-stock prices.

The Importance of Price-Earnings Ratios

Price-earnings ratio (abbreviated as *PF*, *P/E*, and *P-E* and frequently referred to as a stock's *multiple* or *multiplier*) refers to the market price of a stock divided by the issuing company's current earnings per share. A stock that trades at a price of $50.00 per share has a PE of ten when the company is reporting an earnings per share of $5.00. The price-earnings ratio indicates the number of dollars that investors are willing to pay for each dollar of a company's net income.

Investors are willing to pay a high price for a dollar of current earnings when the firm's income is expected to grow at a relatively rapid pace. You are likely to pay a very high price for the stock of a company if you expect earnings of the company to double each year for ten years. Conversely, investors are normally willing to pay only a modest amount per dollar of current earnings when future earnings growth is expected to be moderate.

Suppose a company with 200,000 shares of common stock outstanding is expected to earn $800,000 in the current year. The firm's earnings per share is $4.00 ($800,000/

Figure 9

STOCK MARKET INDICATORS

Numerous stock market indicators attempt to measure the performance of the entire stock market. Stock market indicators are of interest to investors who want to determine how the stock market is performing. Other investors use stock market indicators as a standard against which to measure the performance of their own stock portfolios. The indicators vary in the size of the samples used, in the types of stocks included, in the weighting given to each stock, and in the method of calculation. Some of the most popular stock market indicators are described below.

Dow-Jones Industrial Average (DJIA or The Dow)—The oldest and most frequently quoted indicator is comprised of 30 stocks of some of America's largest and best-known industrial corporations. The Dow is calculated by adding the market prices of the 30 stocks and dividing the sum by a number that takes account of changes in the makeup of the indicator. Dow-Jones publishes separate specialized indicators for utility and transportation stocks.

Standard & Poor's 500 Index (S&P 500)—A popular indicator with financial analysts who consider it to be a more accurate gauge of stock market movements than is the DJIA. The S&P 500 uses the market value (stock price times number of shares outstanding) of 500 stocks and is calculated using a 1941–43 base of 10. Standard & Poor's publishes other specialized indexes.

New York Stock Exchange Index—A series of five indexes that are calculated on a 1965 base of 50 and that use the market values of all the stocks listed on the New York Stock Exchange. The NYSE series is weighted according to each stock's market value so that the stocks of large companies have a large impact on the index.

NASDAQ Series—A series of seven price indicators calculated using all of the domestic over-the-counter stocks on NASDAQ. Each series is calculated using market value weights with a base of 100 in 1971.

Wilshire 5000 Equity Index—A market value weighted index comprised of all the stocks on the New York Stock Exchange and the American Stock Exchange and the most active stocks on the over-the-counter market.

Nikkei-Dow Jones Average—A price weighted index that includes the prices of 225 stocks traded on the Tokyo Stock Exchange.

200,000 shares). If the company's common stock trades at a price of $36.00 per share, the price-earnings ratio is calculated as $36.00/$4.00, or nine times earnings. In other words, investors are willing to pay $9.00 for each $1.00 of the company's current earnings.

Investors are willing to pay $36 for each share of ownership of this firm not only because the company has current earnings of $800,000, but also because of expectations relative to future earnings. Current earnings are most important for what the earnings indicate about a company's future earnings. Thus, current earnings have an impact on a stock's market price by influencing the investment community's forecast of earnings and dividends in future years. If some event alters the forecast, investors are likely to reappraise their judgment of the stock so that the stock's price will change even though current earnings remains unchanged. The bottom line is that a stock's price-earnings ratio is more important for the information the ratio conveys about a firm's future earnings than about its current earnings.

How Stock Values
Are Influenced by Taxes

Taxes on investment income have the effect of reducing the cash flow provided by an investment and reducing the value of the investment. The higher the rate at which the ownership of a particular investment is taxed, the less investors will pay to own that investment. Increased taxes on a business will also result in reduced income for stockholders and a reduced valuation of the business.

There are two types of federal taxes and a variety of state

> Question everything you hear or read about investing. Many people seem to enjoy bragging about how much money they have made investing in common stocks or how much they know about investing in common stocks. Generally, the more they talk the less they know.

and local taxes that affect the returns from stock ownership. Dividends received by stockholders are taxed in the same manner as wages, salaries, and interest income. The federal tax an investor pays on dividend income depends on the investor's tax bracket. There are currently three federal tax brackets: 15 percent, 28 percent, and 31 percent. A taxpayer in the latter tax bracket who receives an additional $1,000 in dividends will pay a tax of $310 (31 percent of $1,000) on the dividends. Someone with a relatively meager income will pay a tax of only $150 (15 percent of $1,000) on the same amount of dividend income.

A second federal tax for an investor who owns common stocks (or virtually any investment) comes into play when shares of stock are sold. The federal government requires that individuals calculate any gains or losses that occur when stock is sold. A gain is the amount by which the proceeds of a sale exceed the cost basis of the stock that is sold. If you purchase 100 shares of Westinghouse common stock at a price of $37 per share and pay a commission of $120, your cost basis will be $3,700 plus $120, or $3,820. If you later sell the stock at a price of $45 per share and pay a commission of $150, you will receive proceeds of $4,500 less $150, or $4,350. The difference of $530 ($4,350 less $3,820) will be taxed at whatever tax rate is appropriate for your total income, subject to a maximum rate of 28 percent.

If you sell several stocks during the same year, gains and losses on the various sales offset one another to arrive at a gain or loss for the year.

State and local governments often levy taxes that parallel federal taxes although at substantially lower rates. Many states require that a resident calculate the state tax liability using adjusted gross income (an amount that includes investment income) from the federal return. A few states levy no income tax on either dividend income or capital gains.

Another tax levied by many state and local governments is an intangible tax. This tax is calculated on the market value of an investment rather than on the income produced by the investment. For example, as a stockholder you may be required to pay an annual tax equal to a percentage of the market value of the stock you own on a particular date. Stock having a market value of $15,000 would entail an annual tax of $150 if a state levies an intangible tax at a rate of one-tenth of 1 percent (.001) of market value.

Taxes have an important impact on investment values because investors tend to evaluate investment returns on an after-tax basis. When taxes are raised, investors will earn lower after-tax returns from stock ownership and will attach less value to owning stock. Reduced taxes have a positive influence on stock values.

CHAPTER 3

How Common Stocks Are Traded

Once common stocks have been issued in the primary market, the securities will begin to trade on the over-the-counter (OTC) market or on organized securities exchanges as investors attempt to sell their shares to other investors. Individual investors must employ the services of brokerage firms to buy and sell stocks in either of these markets. Market makers, who buy and sell securities for their own account and who also match buyers and sellers, are at the heart of the secondary market. Specialists are the market makers on the securities exchanges, and dealers function in the same capacity on the over-the-counter market.

Common stocks are issued by corporations that sell shares of ownership in return for investment capital, which the companies can use to acquire new assets or to repay creditors. Companies do not stand ready to repurchase shares of their own stock from stockholders who for one reason or another decide to sell the shares they have acquired. Corporations that sell stock to investors generally use the funds that are raised to pay for long-term assets such as new buildings and equipment. Because the money has been spent, companies do not have on hand the financial resources necessary to redeem unlimited amounts of their own stock whenever stockholders are in the mood to sell. Thus, an investor who has purchased stock and now wishes to sell the shares must locate another investor who is willing to purchase the stock.

If you become a stockholder of a small company that has a small amount of publicly traded shares and few stockholders, you are likely to encounter a limited market in which to resell the shares. You may find that the company's other stockholders offer the best opportunity for selling your shares. If you know the identities of these other stockholders, you can offer the shares to them. You might also solicit bids for the stock and offer to sell shares to the highest bidder.

While the market system just described may be satisfactory for the infrequent trading of shares in a small company (such as a local bank), the system would not operate effi-

Always view a stock in terms of how it will affect your stock portfolio. Beware of buying additional shares in a stock you already own or acquiring the stock of a company that operates in an industry in which you already hold investments.

ciently for stocks that trade hundreds of thousands or millions of shares on a daily basis. Large and frequent securities transactions are efficiently accomplished only in a highly developed market.

The Role of the Market Maker

If a sufficient number of shares of a stock are available for trading, and enough investors have an interest in buying and selling the stock, a person with sufficient monetary resources may be able to earn a good income by making a market in the stock. A market maker is the person investors turn to when they wish to buy or sell a particular stock. The market maker sometimes functions as a broker who brings together buyers and sellers of the stock, in much the same way that a real estate broker brings together buyers and sellers of homes. For example, investors who own and wish to sell shares of stock in Parrish International contact a market maker in the stock who is likely to be in touch with other investors who have an interest in purchasing shares of Parrish International. Market makers are sometimes unable to locate an investor who will take the opposite side of a trade (i.e., find a buyer to trade with someone who wishes to sell stock or find a seller to trade with someone who wishes to buy stock), in which case the market maker will buy stock from a seller or sell stock to a buyer. In other words, a market maker who is unable to match a buyer with a seller will take the opposite side of the trade him- or herself.

A market maker is the financial world's equivalent of a store owner who buys merchandise for resale and who also accepts merchandise on consignment. In the first instance, the merchant acts as a dealer by paying for and taking possession of the merchandise. When accepting goods on consignment, the merchant does not assume ownership or pay for the merchandise, but rather acts as a broker who will bring potential buyers into contact with the seller. In contrast to a store merchant, who may be willing to hold merchandise for weeks or months before the merchandise is sold, market makers for common stocks typically plan on a very short period of ownership.

By convention, stocks in U.S. markets are priced in eighths of a dollar. For example, a stock may be priced at 42⅜, which translates to a price of $42.375 per share. Similarly, a stock priced at 24¾ trades at a price of $24.75 per share. A quotation of "20 and a quarter" means that a stock is priced at $20.25 per share. When a stock is down by an eighth, the stock has dropped in price by 12.5 cents per share. Likewise, a stock that is up by one and a quarter has increased in price by $1.25 per share compared to some earlier price.

Comparing the Organized Exchanges and the Over-the-Counter Market

Market makers on the New York Stock Exchange and on other organized securities exchanges function in a substantially different environment than market makers on the over-the-counter market. An organized exchange conducts trades in a large number of securities at a particular location, while the over-the-counter market is comprised of thousands of dealers who are scattered across the country and around the globe. A person who performs the market-making function on a securities exchange is at a given location on the floor of the exchange during certain hours of each business day. The exchange market maker interacts on the floor of the exchange with agents of investors who wish to buy and sell stocks handled by the market maker. A market maker on the over-the-counter market is on the other end of a phone line or computer link and could just as well be in Lake Tahoe as in New York City. Neither agents nor investors personally go to an OTC market maker to buy or sell a stock. All of the trading on the OTC market is accomplished by telephone or computer.

Prior to the development of modern communications technology, it was necessary for market makers and investors (or investor's agents) to congregate in the same location each trading day. Investors who were interested in buying or selling a particular stock would always know where to go in order to trade the stock. An investor who could not meet directly with the market maker could employ the services of someone else who had access to this person. With modern communications, dealers can maintain continuous contact with investors, brokers, and other dealers from virtually any location where there is access to the communications system.

The Over-the-Counter Market

Unlike a securities exchange, where stock and bond trading is confined to a particular location, the over-the-counter market is an interconnection of many market makers, actually an interconnection of many markets, that are scattered throughout the country and the world. A firm that acts as a dealer on the over-the-counter market does not possess the financial resources or the personnel to make a market in every OTC stock. Dealers each make markets in a limited number of stocks, some of which are actively traded and some of which are relatively inactive. There may be several different dealers in any given stock, especially if the stock is actively traded. In general, the more trading activity that occurs in a particular stock, the greater the number of dealers that will find it profitable to make a market in that stock. An active OTC stock is likely to have from ten to fifteen market makers. When a stock is relatively inactive, there may be only a single market maker because there isn't sufficient trading volume to entice other dealers to trade in the stock. Over-the-counter stocks with only a single market maker do not qualify for inclusion on the automated quotation system that is carried on broker quotation machines.

OTC market makers operate at both a wholesale and a retail level. At the wholesale level, OTC dealers trade with other industry professionals. Fellow professionals—other dealers who are buying or selling for their own accounts or for resale to others—are quoted better prices by the market maker than are retail customers. At the retail level, OTC market makers deal with retail clients, who are required to pay slightly higher prices to buy stock and receive slightly lower prices when they sell stock.

Suppose you enter an order with your broker to purchase 200 shares of Andersonville Corporation common stock, which is traded on the over-the-counter market. Several market makers are indicated on the quotation machine, and your broker will contact the one who is currently offering the best price. Because you are interested in buying the stock, the best price for you is the lowest price at which the stock is offered for sale. A quotation of "30 bid, offered at 31," indicates that the market maker for Andersonville Corporation stock will purchase shares for $30 and will sell shares for $31. Your broker may either accept the $31 price or choose to make a counteroffer that is somewhat lower than the offered price, say $30.50. The market maker may accept this price or make another counteroffer of $30.75. The price finally arrived at will be the price that is negotiated by the market maker and the broker who represents you.

When you purchase a stock that is traded on the over-the-counter market, you pay the wholesale price plus the broker's markup or fee. If the broker is also a dealer (called a *broker-dealer*) in the stock you purchase, you will pay a price that is higher than the wholesale offering price, which means that the fee is buried in the price you are charged. When you sell an OTC stock, you will receive the wholesale price less the broker's markdown or fee. If your broker makes a market in the stock, you will receive a price that is lower than the wholesale bid.

Market makers adjust the inventory of stock they hold by altering their quotations. For example, a market maker who wants to increase his inventory in a particular stock will increase the bid without altering the offering price. The higher bid should produce an increase in the amount of stock that investors offer to sell the market maker, while an unchanged offering price by the market maker should result in an unchanged demand from investors who wish to buy the stock. A market maker takes many factors into account when setting the bid-and-ask prices for a stock. Several of these factors are discussed later in the chapter in the section about exchange specialists.

Figure 10

SELECT LIST OF STOCKS TRADED ON THE OVER-THE-COUNTER MARKET

Company	Type of Business
Apple Computer	Personal computers
Champion Auto Parts	Vehicle replacement parts
Coors (Adolph)	Brewing and selling beer
Dreyer's Grand Ice Cream	Ice cream
Egghead	Computer software retailer
Fleer Corporation	Bubble gum and sports cards
Justin Industries, Inc.	Building materials, boots, book publishing
Kelly Services, Inc.	Temporary help
La Petite Academy	Day care centers
Mail Boxes Etc.	Postal and packaging services
MCI Communications	Communications
Neutrogena	Skin care products
Republic Pictures	Television programs & distribution
Ryans Family Steak Houses	Operates & franchises restaurants
State Street Boston	Banking & financial services
Topps	Chewing gum and sports cards
Tysons Foods	Poultry and poultry products
Value Line	Investment advisory services
Westmoreland Coal	Coal mining

Organization of the OTC Market

All stocks that are publicly traded but not listed on an organized securities exchange are considered to be traded on the OTC market. Many stocks that are listed on one or more exchanges also trade on the OTC market. So long as someone is willing to make a market, any stock can be traded on the OTC market.

Actually, there are three segments of the OTC market. The National Association of Securities Dealers Automated Quotations National Market System (NASDAQ/NMS) includes nearly 3,000 stocks that have substantial trading activity, several market makers, and a relatively large market value. Most newspapers that provide OTC price quotations usually limit the list to stocks that are part of the National Market System. Most papers include only the more active stocks included in the National Market System.

The regular NASDAQ system includes another 2,400 stocks that meet certain minimum standards, including at least 300 shareholders, 100,000 outstanding shares, $2 million of assets, and $1 million of capital and surplus. The third segment of the OTC market includes approximately 11,000 stocks that do not meet the standards for being included in the regular NASDAQ system. These stocks are quoted in the daily "pink sheets" published by the National Quotation Bureau, but the stocks are not carried by the NASDAQ system, which can be accessed by quotation machines.

Organization of a Securities Exchange

An organized securities exchange is a privately owned and operated marketplace for the trading of selected securities. A securities exchange is owned by the members who hold *seats* on the exchange. Owning a seat allows the member to participate in setting policy for the exchange and to engage in the trading of securities on the exchange floor. Not all exchange members perform the same functions. Approximately a quarter of the members are specialists, who perform the market-making function for stocks that have been listed on the exchange. Trading in a stock is assigned to a particular specialist when the stock is listed.

A large number of exchange members act as commission brokers, who execute orders to buy and sell securities for customers of a member firm. Other members are floor brokers, who operate independently to assist commission brokers when trading activity is unusually heavy. A relatively small number of exchange members are registered traders, who buy and sell securities for their own account.

A securities exchange has a limited number of memberships (the NYSE has 1,366 members), which means that someone interested in acquiring a seat must locate a current member who is willing to sell one. The value of a seat is subject to supply-and-demand pressures that are largely determined by the profitability of being an exchange member. This, in turn, is primarily a function of the volume of trading on the exchange. Seats on a securities exchange tend to bring increased prices during periods of relatively high trading volume.

The organized exchanges do not each provide markets in all securities. The stocks of the majority of large, nationally known companies have their primary market at the New York Stock Exchange (NYSE), although many of the same stocks are also traded on one or more of the regional exchanges. The organized exchanges also make markets in a

> Beware of a broker who advises you to do a lot of buying and selling of common stocks. A lot of in-and-out trading generally results in more income for the broker than for you.

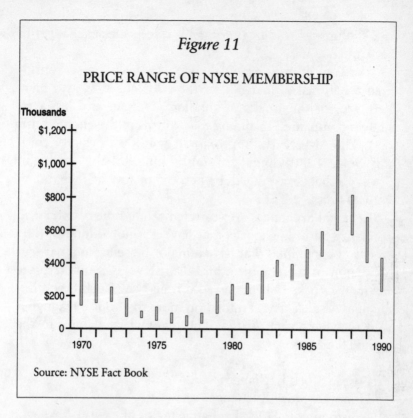

Figure 11

PRICE RANGE OF NYSE MEMBERSHIP

Source: NYSE Fact Book

limited number of corporate bonds, but most bonds are traded on the over-the-counter market.

The NYSE, also called the *Big Board,* is by far the largest organized securities exchange in the United States and serves as the primary marketplace for the stocks of corporate giants such as General Motors, Westinghouse, Procter & Gamble, Southern Company, Exxon, and General Electric. At the beginning of 1992 the NYSE listed 2,284 securities issues, including 110 non-U.S. issues. The New York Stock Exchange accounts for approximately 85 percent of the total volume of trading on organized securities exchanges in the United States.

The American Stock Exchange (AMEX) is also considered a national exchange, but the AMEX serves as a marketplace for the stocks of smaller, younger, and less well known companies, including many firms in the energy business. The AMEX lists approximately 1,000 stocks for trading. Since 1980 annual trading volume on the American Stock Exchange averaged 10 percent or less of the trading volume on the NYSE.

Regional exchanges are scattered around the country and specialize in trading stocks that have a regional interest (i.e., stocks of companies that have a major presence in a particular region of the country), and also serve as a marketplace for many stocks that are listed on the New York Stock Exchange. A stock that is traded on more than one exchange is said to have a *dual listing*. The regional exchanges in the United States are:

Boston Stock Exchange
Honolulu Stock Exchange
Intermountain Stock Exchange (Salt Lake City)
Midwest Stock Exchange (Chicago)
Pacific Stock Exchange (Los Angeles and San Francisco)
PBW Exchange (Philadelphia-Baltimore-Washington)
Spokane Stock Exchange

Each securities exchange establishes its own standards for stocks to be listed for trading. The New York Stock Exchange imposes the most restrictive standards. In order to have its stock listed for trading on the NYSE, a company must have:

- at least 2,000 holders of one hundred shares or more;
- $18,000,000 or more in the market value of publicly held shares;
- net tangible assets of at least $18,000,000;
- a minimum of 1,100,000 of publicly held shares; and
- demonstrated earning power over the past three years.

The NYSE has also established standards for a stock to maintain its listing on the exchange. A company must pay an exchange both an initial sum and an annual fee in order to have its stock listed for trading.

The Specialist System

Specialists are at the heart of trading on an organized securities exchange. The specialist acts as the market maker for specific securities (generally fifteen to twenty different issues) that are listed on the exchange and that have been assigned to that particular specialist by a committee of exchange members. No other specialists on the exchange act as market makers in the same stocks, although the stocks may be traded on other exchanges and on the over-the-counter market. It is the specialist's job to provide liquidity (make it easy for investors to buy and sell) for stocks that have been assigned to him or her.

Specialists are stationed at trading desks (called *posts*) on the floor of the stock exchange. Specialists remain at their respective posts each day so that a member who is interested in entering into a transaction for a particular stock will know the exact location on the exchange floor where that stock is traded.

Figure 12

NYSE FLOOR

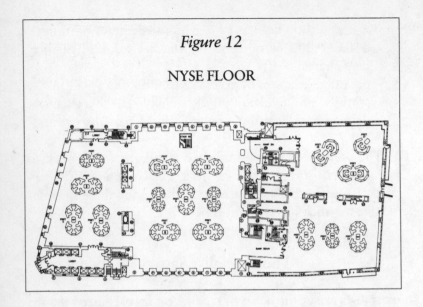

Specialists frequently act as brokers who bring together buyers and sellers, while at other times they serve as dealers who buy for or sell from their own portfolios in order to maintain orderly markets. Specialists perform as brokers when commission brokers bring customer orders with price limits that do not allow the orders to be executed in the current market. For example, an investor might place an order to purchase 200 shares of Goodyear common stock at a maximum price of $37 per share at a time when Goodyear stock is trading for $39 per share. Rather than constantly monitor the stock price in case there is a decline to $37, the commission broker leaves the order with the specialist, who makes note of the order so that a transaction will occur if market forces eventually cause the price of the stock to decline to the specified price or less.

A specialist must perform as a dealer (i.e., must buy and

sell shares for the specialist's personal account) in assigned stocks when there is a lack of investor supply and demand. A member order to sell stock at a time when there is lack of investor demand for the stock will require that the specialist buy the stock for his or her own account. When there is a lack of supply for a stock, the specialist will sell shares of the stock from his or her own account. The specialist's job is to act as a stabilizing force in the assigned stocks by being a buyer when there is strong investor selling pressure and a seller when there is strong investor buying pressure. In other words, specialists are often called upon to provide a fair and orderly market in their assigned stocks by going against market forces.

The specialist takes into account the forces of supply and demand when quoting a price for a particular stock. If there are many investor orders to buy a stock but few investor orders to sell the stock, the specialist is likely to raise the bid-and-ask prices for the stock in order to alter investor orders. The higher ask price (the price at which the specialist stands ready to sell shares of stock) will deter some investors from buying stock at the same time that a higher bid price (the price at which the specialist stands ready to buy stock) should stimulate additional investor interest in selling the stock. The specialist adjusts a stock's price quotation upward or downward until investor demand and supply for the stock are brought into balance.

Don't get caught up in short-term price movements of stocks that you buy. Don't become discouraged when you buy a stock that subsequently drops by a point or two, and don't become too excited when you buy a stock that soon climbs in price by several points.

The specialist's bid-and-ask quotations for an assigned stock are also influenced by his or her current position in the stock (i.e., how many shares of the stock the specialist owns or owes) in comparison to the desired position in the stock. A specialist who is interested in decreasing the amount of stock that is owned will reduce the bid-and-ask quotations in order to attract more buyers and fewer sellers. A specialist who would like to increase the position size in an assigned stock will increase the bid-and-ask quotations.

Much of the trading at specialist posts is accomplished with an electronic system that transmits orders from member firm offices to the specialist. On the New York Stock Exchange the automatic system is the *Super DOT* system, DOT being an acronym for *Designated Order Turnaround*. DOT and similar systems at other exchanges are designed to provide for the automatic execution of the large number of modest-size orders that would otherwise require much of the specialists' time and clog up the trading system.

The specialist has two sources of income. On customer orders that are left for execution, the specialist earns a fee from the commission broker. A specialist who is a market maker in active stocks such as Texaco, Coca-Cola, and American Telephone & Telegraph will earn a substantial income from the brokerage side of the business. When an assigned stock is relatively inactive, the specialist must be an active dealer and will attempt to earn an income from intelligent trading of the stock. Intelligent trading means that the specialist profits from correctly anticipating future market movements. When one of the specialist's stocks is experiencing a price decline that is judged to be temporary, the specialist may decide to increase the size of his or her position in the stock in order to profit from the expected upturn.

Conversely, a specialist is likely to reduce the size of a position of a stock that he or she believes will soon fall in price.

The specialist is assisted in the task of profitably trading a stock by having access to privileged information regarding orders that have been left with him or her to be executed at prices away from the current market. The specialist will know if there are a large number of orders to purchase shares of an assigned stock in the event the price of the stock dips slightly. Such knowledge allows the specialist to take a relatively large position in the stock (acquire a large number of shares of the stock) without fear that the stock price will be subject to a major decline.

Types of Orders

You can choose among several kinds of orders when you buy or sell shares of common stock. The type of order that should be used depends primarily upon your goals. When you invest for the long term, you are less likely to be concerned about buying shares at the very lowest price or selling shares at the very highest price. A long investment horizon makes an extra profit of 25 cents per share seem relatively unimportant. On the other hand, you will be very interested in obtaining the best possible price when you are attempting to earn relatively small profits on many different transactions. You can place the following types of orders.

Market Order—A market order is an order to buy or to sell a stock at the best available price at the time the order arrives on the floor of the exchange. No price or time limit is specified on the order. When you wish to buy stock, the best available price is the lowest possible price. When you wish to sell stock, the best available price is the highest possible price. In truth, the market order will be executed at whatever the prevailing price happens to be at the time the order reaches the floor of the exchange.

A market order is used when you wish either to buy or sell stock and are not concerned about the exact price at which an execution takes place. You may decide that you would like to become a stockholder of Woolworth Corporation. You check the morning paper and observe that the firm's stock closed the previous day at a price of $35 per share. You call your broker, who informs you that the stock is currently trading up an eighth (higher by 12.5 cents per share) from yesterday's closing price and that the current quotation is $35.00 bid, $35.25 ask. If you place a market order at this time, chances are you will pay the ask, or $35.25 per share for Woolworth stock. The broker's commission is added to the amount you must pay. You feel comfortable placing a market order because you are not particularly concerned about whether you end up paying $35.25, $35.37, or even $35.50 per share for Woolworth common stock.

When you place a market order you know that the order will be executed, but you are unsure about the exact price of the execution. Using a market order is most likely to produce an acceptable outcome when you are buying or selling an active stock that exhibits only small price movements. A market order may result in a disappointing outcome (i.e., paying too high a price when purchasing the stock or receiving too low a price when selling the stock) when you buy or sell a lightly traded stock that is subject to sudden price movements.

Limit Order—A limit order is an order to buy stock with

If you sell stock and must mail the certificate, you should use registered mail. Transfer agents generally recommend that you insure the contents for 2 percent of the value of the stock you are sending because this will be the cost of obtaining a new certificate in the event that your certificate is lost.

a specified maximum purchase price or to sell stock with a specified minimum selling price. The price restriction included in a limit order means that an investor will not receive less than the specified price when the stock is sold and will not pay more than the specified price when the stock is purchased. The problem with using a limit order is that there is a chance the stock may not trade at the specified price and that the order will therefore not be executed.

Suppose you have studied the daily price activity of Woolworth stock during the past several months and have noticed that it is not unusual for the stock to trade over a price range of 75 cents to $1.50 during a typical day. In other words, the stock's price is likely to vary as little as 75 cents and as much as $1.50 during a typical trading day. You expect this price variation to continue and decide to place a limit order to buy the stock at a maximum price of $34.50. You hope that the stock price will temporarily dip to $34.50 or less so that your order will be executed at a price that produces a savings of 50 cents per share, compared to the current $35.00 price. The risk of this strategy is that Woolworth's stock price may begin an immediate upward movement without declining to $34.50, in which case you will have to pay more than you intended when you eventually purchase the stock or else you will be without a stock that you wanted to own.

A limit order that cannot be immediately executed because the market price of the stock differs from the price specified in the order is left with the specialist, who will execute the order if and when the price moves to the specified level. At any particular time a specialist will have many limit orders that have been left by commission brokers because customer orders could not be executed at the prevailing stock price at the time the order arrived at the exchange floor. Limit orders to sell shares at prices higher than the stock's current price (limit orders to sell at prices lower than the current price will have already been executed) provide the specialist with an indication of the potential supply of shares in case the stock price begins rising. Limit orders placed by investors who want to buy shares at prices that are lower than the stock's current price provide the specialist with an indication of the demand for the stock in case the stock price declines.

When you place a limit order, your broker will ask you how long the order is to remain active in case it cannot be executed immediately. The choice for most investors is between a *day-only* order or a *good-till-canceled* (GTC) order, although virtually any time frame can be specified. A day-only order is automatically canceled at the end of trading on the day the order is entered. You must reenter the order the following morning if you are still interested in undertaking the transaction. A good-till-canceled order remains active either until the order is executed (i.e., a transaction occurs) or until you cancel the order.

Stop Order—A less frequently used order is a stop order, which can be used to protect a profit or limit a loss. Like limit orders, stop orders are left with the specialist to execute when and if the stock price reaches a specified level. A stop order to buy becomes a market order when the price of the stock reaches the stop price or a price higher than the stop price. A stop order to buy is used when you intend to purchase a stock only at a price that is *higher* than the current price. For example, at a time when Ford common stock trades at $40 per share, you might place a stop order to purchase 300 shares of Ford if and when the price rises to $43.

A stop order to sell a stock becomes a market order when the price of the stock reaches the specified price or lower. A stop order to sell is used when you intend to sell, but only if the stock price falls to a specified level that is lower than the stock's current market price. Suppose you purchased Ford stock at a price of $30 per share several years ago. The stock now trades at $40, but you are concerned that a large price decline may erase your paper profit. You may decide to place a stop order to sell the stock at a specified price of $37 or less. In the event the stock begins to decline, the order will become a market order when and if the price hits $37. In this instance, you have used a stop order to protect a profit. The risk of using this type of order is that the stock price may temporarily dip to the specified price, thereby causing the stop order to be executed just before the stock resumes an upward price movement.

Short Sale—A short sale is the sale of borrowed stock. The purpose of a short sale is to profit from an expected decline in the price of a stock that is sold short. In this type of transaction you sell borrowed stock and later purchase an equal amount of the same stock (called a *covering transaction*), which is used to replace the shares that were borrowed. If the shares are purchased at a price that is lower than the price at which the stock was sold, you will earn a profit from the transaction.

Suppose that Corning common stock currently trades for $35 per share, a price that you feel is too high. You phone your broker and place an order to sell short 500 shares of Corning stock at $35. Six months later, when your prognosis proves accurate and Corning stock has fallen to $25 per share, you repurchase and replace the borrowed stock. Your profit on the two transactions equals the proceeds from the sale ($17,500 less brokerage commissions) less the cost basis of the subsequent purchase ($12,500 plus brokerage commissions).

Your broker will take care of borrowing the stock for a short sale, and there is no additional charge or commission involved for this type of transaction. In some instances the brokerage firm will already hold the stock you wish to sell short in its own portfolio, while at other times the brokerage firm will use stock that is owned by another customer of the firm. Brokerage firms are sometimes required to borrow stock from another firm.

Certain rules apply to a short sale, although the regulations do not make it difficult for an investor to undertake such a transaction. For example, stocks can only be sold short when the previous price change in the stock was in an upward direction (called an uptick). Many investors have no interest in short selling, either because they don't know that such a transaction is possible or because they feel uneasy about selling something that they don't own. Nonetheless, short selling is popular with some investors, and stock exchange specialists regularly engage in this type of transaction. Keep in mind that you can suffer substantial losses if a stock begins increasing in price after you sell the stock short. In fact, it is possible to lose a greater amount than you originally invested.

CHAPTER 4

Selecting a
Broker and a
Brokerage Firm

B rokerage firms provide investors with a
link to common stocks in both the primary and secondary markets. In addition to
executing orders, most brokers dispense advice on which stocks to buy and sell and supply information on various investment topics.
Increasing numbers of investors are turning to
discount brokerage firms that provide security
transactions at a substantial commission savings compared to the commissions charged by
many full-service firms.

An investor who wishes to purchase the stock of a company that will be issuing shares as part of an initial public offering and an investor who is interested in acquiring shares that are traded on the New York Stock Exchange must both normally employ the services of a retail brokerage firm. Brokerage firms have access to both the primary market, where new stock issues are sold, and the secondary market, where outstanding shares of stock are traded among investors. Brokerage firms are the intermediaries through which individual and institutional investors are able to acquire and dispose of securities.

Although brokerage firms all provide for the execution of investor orders to buy and sell securities, not all brokerage companies are exactly alike. Brokerage firms offer differing services, levy different fees, charge different interest rates on customer borrowing, and have different employees. This last factor may turn out to be the most important consideration for most investors, although many individuals don't recognize this fact until after they have chosen a firm. A good broker will call your attention to new products and undervalued stocks, will help untangle problems you may have with your account or with the firm, and will provide current research materials you may be unaware of. A broker who takes an interest in your financial well-being and who offers substantive financial advice is a good person to have in your corner.

What Brokerage Firms Do

First and foremost, brokerage companies provide executions of customer orders to buy and sell securities in both the primary market and the secondary market. Virtually all brokerage firms will provide for transactions for any type of

Selecting a Broker and a Brokerage Firm

Full-service brokerage firms will sometimes discount their commissions if you ask. It is a good policy to inquire about the possibility of a lower commission before you place an order. You certainly don't have anything to lose.

publicly traded security in whatever market the security is traded. Likewise, all brokerage firms will typically accept any of the several types of restrictive orders—limit orders, stop orders, stop limit orders, and so forth. A brokerage firm will take care of your order regardless of whether a stock is traded on the New York Stock Exchange, on one of the many regional exchanges, or on the over-the-counter market, although some firms charge slightly different fees depending on the market in which an order is executed.

Brokerage firms offer several services in addition to their primary function of executing customer orders to buy and sell securities. Many brokerage offices house a library of investment materials, where customers may pass the day studying stock reports, company research, investment opinions, stock price charts, and investment periodicals. A decreasing number of brokerage offices house a quotation board, along with an area where customers may sit and observe the reporting of transactions on the New York Stock Exchange and the American Stock Exchange. Most brokerage firms are also helpful about providing groups and clubs with speakers who will discuss the virtues of investing.

The majority of brokerage firms employ brokers who make it part of their job to advise you on your investment decisions. The brokers are likely to offer recommendations on stocks to buy, stocks to sell, and whether you should continue to hold stocks you already own. Many brokers are also willing to advise you on an overall investment program that they judge to be compatible with your financial goals.

Brokerage firms typically handle orders for a wide range of investment products, including common stocks, preferred stocks, corporate bonds, money market funds, government securities, municipal bonds, mutual funds, investment trusts, futures contracts, partnerships, options, foreign securities, annuities, and a variety of insurance lines. Many brokerage firms will arrange for a loan on your house, and all brokerage companies will provide loans that use your securities as collateral. Certain brokerage accounts even include the option of allowing customers to use a credit card to access cash and borrowing power within an account.

Opening a Brokerage Account

When you walk into a brokerage office with the intent of opening an account, you will be met by a receptionist who is familiar with the firm's brokers. Now is the time for you to indicate the type of broker you would prefer to work with. Would you rather do business with a young and aggressive broker who is likely to lead you into purchasing fairly risky securities that offer an opportunity for large profits, or would you prefer a broker with many years of experience, who will tend to steer clients toward conservative investments? Despite the descriptions used here, age is not always an accurate guide to the types of investments a broker will pitch. Are you more comfortable working with a male or a female broker? If your primary interest is buying stocks that produce substantial dividend income, you should ask the receptionist if any of the brokers have a special interest in these particular stocks. If you are mainly interested in buying tax-exempt municipal bonds, you should request a broker who is most likely to be up to snuff on this specialized security. Although most brokers are versed in a wide variety of products, there is no way that any broker can keep up with all aspects of each of the products that brokerage companies offer.

If you find that your investment interests or personality are not compatible with the broker who services your account, you can always request that your account be transferred to another broker in the same office. If you decide for whatever reason that you would rather have your account at a different brokerage firm, there is a relatively simple process whereby the securities in your account can be transferred to another firm. If there are no assets in your account, you need merely open an account at a different firm and quit doing business at your existing firm.

When you meet with a broker, keep in mind that the broker will earn an income from having you as a customer only when you buy and sell securities. This arrangement has a built-in conflict of interest because it is to the broker's advantage that you trade securities frequently so long as you don't become unhappy enough to move your account to another broker or another firm. Excessive trading of securities in a customer's account is known as *churning*. You should

Consider opening accounts at both a full-service brokerage firm and a discount brokerage firm. Having an account at each type of firm allows you to take advantage of the best features of each. If you make substantial investments in common stocks, you may want to have even more than two accounts.

look for a broker who will look after your long-term interests rather than his or her short-term interests.

It is not difficult to open a brokerage account. In many respects the procedure is similar to opening a bank account. You will be required to complete some paperwork that includes your address, age, employer, spouse, and investment objective. You are likely to be asked for a bank reference and for brokerage firms with which you have previously had an account. If you have an interest in trading options (highly volatile and risky investments that should be avoided by all but experienced investors), you will be required to complete additional forms that require more detailed information.

Opening a Brokerage
Account by Mail

It is not mandatory that you open an account in person. Many investors maintain a brokerage account without having once visited the office that holds their account. You may live in a rural area that does not have a local brokerage firm. Perhaps you prefer to maintain an account outside your hometown because you are uncomfortable with local brokerage employees having knowledge of your financial affairs. Regardless of the reason, you are not required to appear in person to open an account. Simply phone or write the firm where you have chosen to open an account and request the proper forms. Many firms send prospective clients an introductory package that includes an account application along with information about the firm's services and fees.

National versus
Regional Brokerage Firms

Some investors feel more comfortable when they deal with a major brokerage firm that has many offices and that advertises extensively in newspapers and on television. Size and name familiarity provide these investors with a sense of security that they are unable to obtain from a small brokerage firm. Other investors choose to open an account at the local branch of a regional brokerage firm, where they are able to drop in to visit and talk with their broker and other friends and where they can obtain current research material. If you feel that you need to establish a relationship with a broker, it is probably best to open an account locally. If you make your own investment decisions and use a broker primarily to have your orders executed, it makes little difference whether you choose one of the large national brokerage firms or a smaller, regional firm.

A regional brokerage firm is likely to concentrate on providing its customers with research and information about the stocks of businesses that are located in your region of the country. Providing specialized research is one of the ways that regional firms differentiate themselves from national brokerage firms, which mainly follow companies that have a national presence. You may or may not consider having access to this type of research to be important, depending on the kinds of stocks you plan to purchase. Another consideration in choosing among brokerage firms of different size is that large brokerage companies sometimes offer products or services that are not available at many regional firms. For example, the comprehensive asset management account discussed later in this chapter is a costly product that is offered only by the larger brokerage firms.

Discount Brokerage Firms

Prior to 1975 the fee charged for a stock trade of a given size was the same at nearly all brokerage firms. That is, you would pay exactly the same commission whether you placed an order to buy stock with a small local firm, a nearby regional firm, or a distant national firm. Pressure from institutional investors and the federal government eventually prodded the industry to end the practice of price fixing and move into an era in which brokerage firms competed for investor business on the basis of commissions. In certain instances investors can now negotiate commissions on large orders.

Scrapping fixed commission rates brought a new competitiveness, and an entirely new segment of the brokerage industry was born. *Discount brokers* generally offer substantial commission reductions compared to the standard fees charged by full-service firms such as Merrill Lynch and Paine Webber. At the same time that discounters offer reduced commission rates, these firms do not spend money on research, and they are not staffed to provide customers with investment advice. Most discount brokerage firms are in business to provide executions and discounted fees to customers who make their own investment decisions.

If a mutual fund salesperson says that a mutual fund does not have a sales fee, make sure that the fund also does not have a fee to redeem shares or an annual 12b-1 fee.

Two fairly distinct segments of the discount brokerage industry have evolved. One segment is comprised of firms that engage in substantial advertising, have offices scattered across the country, and offer all types of financial services and products with the exception of investment advice. Firms in this category include Charles Schwab, Quick & Reilly, and Fidelity Investor Services. These large discount brokerage firms sell an extensive variety of investment products and have a relatively high overhead. They offer most investors the potential for sizable commission savings compared to the commissions charged by large full-service firms, but the fees of the large discount firms may be substantially higher than the commissions that investors can obtain from other discounters that have a lower overhead.

The second portion of the discount brokerage industry is comprised of firms that do little else than buy and sell securities at very low commissions. These bare-bones discounters normally operate from a single office via a toll-free telephone number. Their low overhead permits these firms to offer investors very low commissions.

Some discount brokerage firms have commission schedules that are established primarily on the basis of the number of shares in a customer's order. These firms charge fees that are largely independent of the price of the stock that a customer trades. The commission for trading 500 shares of a $15 stock is approximately the same as the commission for trading 500 shares of a $45 stock, despite the fact that the second trade has three times the market value of the first. Other discounters set commission charges on the basis of the dollar value of a transaction. Firms of this type charge approximately the same commission to trade 200 shares of a $50 stock as to trade 500 shares of a $20 stock.

If you believe you will be mostly interested in low-priced stocks, you are likely to save on commissions by seeking a discount broker that sets its fees on the basis of the market value rather than the number of shares in a transaction. Of course, you can follow the lead of many investors and open two accounts, one at each type of firm.

Figure 13

ABBREVIATED LIST OF
DISCOUNT BROKERAGE FIRMS

Brown & Company
20 Winthrop Square
Boston, MA 02110
1-800-225-6707

Fidelity Investments
  Discount Brokerage
161 Devonshire Street
Boston, MA 02110
1-800-544-5115

Quick & Reilly
120 Wall Street
New York, NY 10005
1-800-222-0513

Charles Schwab & Co.,
  Inc.
101 Montgomery Street
San Francisco, CA
94104
1-800-648-5300

Seaport Securities
19 Rector Street
New York, NY 10006
1-800-732-7678

Muriel Siebert & Co.,
  Inc.
444 Madison Avenue
New York, NY 10022
1-800-872-0711

StockCross
One Washington Mall
Boston, MA 02108
1-800-225-6196

Waterhouse Securities,
  Inc.
44 Wall Street
New York, NY 10005
1-800-765-5185

York Securities, Inc.
160 Broadway,
  East Building
New York, NY 10038
1-800-221-3154

Choosing Between a Discount Firm and a Full-Service Firm

Now that brokerage firms are free to establish their own commission schedules, it has become important for an investor who is opening a brokerage account to investigate a firm's commission rates. There is nothing wrong with asking a brokerage firm about its commission structure or, at least, the commissions that the firm would charge for the type(s) of transactions you are most likely to be making.

Neophyte investors are likely to need the advice and research that are provided by brokers at a full-service firm even though the commission charges will be higher than those that would be levied by discount firms. An additional $30 or $40 in commissions to buy one hundred shares of stock is money well spent if an investor, left to his or her own devices, would end up selecting stocks at random or would invest on the basis of tips provided by friends.

Be aware that most discount brokers have a minimum transaction charge in the range of $35 to $50, which makes some stock transactions less expensive to undertake at full-service firms that have no minimum commissions. You should also be aware that full-service firms are sometimes willing to negotiate the commission on a trade. The chance of obtaining a discount off the normal fee from a full-service firm is a function of the size of the trade and the amount of business you conduct with the firm.

The Typical Brokerage Account

When you open an account you will be asked whether the account is to be in your name only or in your name plus one or more other names. A joint account establishes joint ownership between two or more individuals, such as a husband and wife or a parent and child. Most joint accounts are established as "joint tenancy with rights of survivorship," which means that if one owner dies, the property in the account automatically passes to the other account holder(s). A more unusual type of joint account is one known as "tenants in common," in which the property of a deceased owner passes according to the deceased's will or, without a will, to the deceased's estate rather than to the other owners of the account.

Brokerage firms are required to provide you with monthly account statements during months in which there is investment activity in your account; at other times most firms mail quarterly statements to their customers. Brokerage statements indicate securities and cash being held in the account along with any investment activity that took place during the time covered by the statement. Securities being held in the account are listed and generally valued as of the statement date. Account activity includes security purchases, security sales, credits of dividends or interest from securities being held in the account, cash deposited into the account, securities deposited into the account, cash payments made to the account holder, and charges against the account during the period covered by the statement.

There are normally no charges involved in opening a brokerage account, although some firms now levy an annual charge on accounts in which securities are being held but in which there has been no investment activity (i.e., no purchases or sales of securities) during the year. Typical charges range from $25 to $50 annually. Account maintenance charges are not levied by all firms, and you should inquire about a firm's policy regarding account charges when you open an account. In early 1992 Merrill Lynch announced that the firm would begin charging an annual fee on all accounts, including those accounts in which there was investment activity.

Transactions to buy or sell stock nearly always require a settlement date that follows by five business days the date of the transaction. In other words, the parties involved in a transaction have five business days (generally, one week) to deliver the payment and the securities. If you purchase stock on Monday, payment for the purchase will normally be required by the following Monday. When you sell stock, delivery of the stock certificate will generally be required by the following Monday, at which time you will receive the proceeds from the sale.

Dividends and interest that are paid on securities being held in your account will be credited to your account. These amounts are normally forwarded by check to you on the first of the month following receipt of the payments. For example, a $100 dividend paid on stock being held in your account will result in the brokerage firm sending you a $100 check early in the month that follows the date on which the dividend was credited to the account. You can also phone your broker and request that a credit balance (cash held in the account) be sent immediately, although such an exercise may become tiresome for both you and your broker if it occurs every time your account is credited with a dividend.

Avoid doing business with a broker who recommends stocks without first finding out about your resources and goals. A particular stock is not an appropriate holding for all investors, regardless of how undervalued the stock may seem.

Some brokerage accounts automatically sweep cash balances into a money market fund so that there is no need to send customers a monthly check. Automatic reinvestment of cash balances is a considerable advantage because you do not have to wait a month to reinvest cash payments that are made to your brokerage account. You should inquire about a brokerage firm's policy regarding the cash balances in an account when you shop for a brokerage firm.

If you are willing to turn over all investment decisions to your broker, you may be interested in opening a *discretionary account*. A discretionary account requires that you sign a power of attorney, giving your broker the authority to buy and sell securities for the account without first seeking your approval. A discretionary account can be either an individual account or a joint account, and it can be either a cash account or a margin account (see below). A discretionary account requires that you have a great deal of confidence in your broker, and for most investors, opening such an account is an unwise decision.

Choosing Between a Cash Account and a Margin Account

One of your decisions at the time you open a brokerage account is to choose between a cash account and a margin account. The cash account is the most common type of brokerage account maintained by individual investors. It requires that you pay in full on the settlement date when securities are purchased and that you promptly deliver securities that are sold. In other words, a cash account requires that you maintain your account on a current basis.

A margin account allows you to use credit to pay for a portion of securities that you purchase. If you choose to open a margin account, borrowing will be automatically arranged by your brokerage firm when you purchase securities. The maximum proportion of a transaction that may be borrowed—currently 50 percent—is established by the Federal Reserve Board. If you open a margin account, you will be required to sign an agreement that pledges your stock as collateral for loans the brokerage firm arranges. Stock that is pledged as collateral must remain in the account. Most brokerage firms will also require that you sign an additional form that permits the firm to lend stock being held in your account.

Interest charges for a margin loan are calculated on the basis of an account's debit balance (the amount borrowed) and the interest rate in effect during the period the loan is outstanding. Debit balances may be repaid at any time in full or in part, and there is no specific date on which the entire loan must be repaid. Interest charges to your account are adjusted downward for payments that reduce the amount of a loan. The interest rate charged on a margin loan is a variable rate that is determined by the *call money rate,* a short-term interest rate that is approximately equal to a bank's prime rate. Brokerage firms generally charge a slightly lower interest rate when large amounts are borrowed. There is no interest charge when a margin account has no debit balance, and the account will not incur any special charges that are different from those levied against a cash account.

A margin account permits you to purchase more stock than you could afford if you were required to pay cash for the full amount of the purchase. A margin account also allows you to borrow money against securities that are being held in your account. Funds borrowed from a margin account may be used in any way you see fit. For example, if you have securities in your margin account that are not currently being used as collateral for a loan, you may decide to pay for a new car by borrowing from the brokerage firm rather than by taking out an auto loan at a bank or credit union.

One of the great risks of maintaining a margin account is the additional losses than can result from using borrowed money to buy securities. If you purchase twice as much stock using a margin account as you would purchase with a cash account, you will end up with larger profits or losses. The magnification of profits and losses makes buying on margin a relatively risky undertaking.

The Comprehensive
Asset Management Account

In the late 1970s Merrill Lynch introduced a new and innovative brokerage account that incorporated nearly all of the financial services needed by an individual investor. Merrill Lynch's trademarked Cash Management Account (CMA) brought together into a single all-inclusive brokerage account a checking account, margin loan availability, debit card, money market fund, safekeeping for securities, and automatic investment of any cash credited to the account. Customers opening a CMA are required to deposit cash or securities with a market value of at least $20,000. Although Merrill Lynch secured a big jump on the industry with the Cash Management Account, other major brokerage companies and a number of large commercial banks have since introduced virtually identical accounts under a variety of trademarked names.

Keep your brokerage confirmation slips and maintain a record of your stock transactions. You will need information regarding the prices and commissions you pay in order to calculate the taxes due when you sell shares of stock.

Any cash that is deposited in an asset management account or that is received from dividends and interest on securities held in the account is automatically swept into a money market fund. Automatic reinvestment means that any cash in your account will immediately be put to work earning a return. Soon after the account is opened, you will receive checks and a debit card or credit card that allows you to access funds in the account. When you write a check or use the credit card, just enough of the money market fund is liquidated to pay the bill. The advantage of this feature is that funds invested in the money market fund continue to earn interest income until the check or credit card charge is presented for payment. If the money market fund balance is insufficient to take care of the charges that are presented, a loan is automatically made for the balance of the charges. As a holder of an asset management account, you can write checks and use the debit or credit card to access the account's borrowing power up to the allowable amount based on the value of securities held in the account.

Brokerage firms typically charge from $50 to $100 annually to maintain an asset management account. The features of each firm's accounts differ slightly. For example, some firms provide a debit card (purchase amounts using the card are immediately deducted from the account) with the account; a credit card (charges are deducted from the account at the end of the month) is available only at an added fee. Other firms include a credit card as a standard part of the account. Some firms sweep small cash balances into the money market fund weekly, while other firms sweep these balances daily. Some firms require less than $20,000 to open one of these accounts, and not all firms charge $100 a year to maintain the account. If you are interested in an asset management account, you should shop around for the brokerage firm that offers the best combination of features and price.

All-inclusive asset management accounts are primarily designed for active investors who have substantial financial assets. Still, the advantages of having such an account may be worth the nominal annual cost for even an occasional investor, especially given today's high cost of maintaining a regular checking account.

Keeping Stock in Street Name

When you open a brokerage account you must decide whether to have certificates for stock that you purchase mailed to you (referred to as having the securities *delivered*) or to have the brokerage firm retain the securities in your account (referred to as keeping the securities in *street name*). Choosing to have securities delivered means that you must provide for safekeeping of the certificates. Replacing a lost certificate involves a rather lengthy process that requires you to pay a fee equal to approximately 2 percent of the market value of the stock represented by the certificate. Replacing a lost certificate for 500 shares of a stock that trades at a price of $20 per share will entail a cost of approximately $200. On the other hand, having possession of a certificate means that you are free to sell the stock at the brokerage firm of your choice.

Having stock you purchase kept in street name frees you from worry about safekeeping for the certificates. It also allows you to sell your stock without being required to deliver a certificate to your broker. Other than the potential for incurring an annual fee for having an inactive account, there is normally no additional charge for having a brokerage firm maintain custody of your stock. In fact, Wall Street institutions have been trying for years to convince investors to have certificates left in street name in order to reduce the effort and expense of continually transferring securities. Certain new bonds are being issued with the restriction that the bonds can *only* be credited to an investor's account. In other words, certain securities cannot be delivered to an investor.

If you decide to leave stock in street name, you can request that your broker have the shares delivered at any time. If you specify that stock be kept in street name but later change your mind, you can request your broker to have the stock delivered out of the account. If you later decide to change brokerage firms, you can provide written authorization for your new firm to have the securities being held at your existing account transferred to the new account.

Safety of Assets Kept
in a Brokerage Account

Brokerage firms are members of the Securities Investors Protection Corporation (SIPC), a government-sponsored, privately funded organization that protects the cash and securities in a customer account to a maximum of

$500,000. SIPC insurance limits coverage for cash losses to a maximum of $100,000.

SIPC was formed in 1970 amid widespread concern about the financial stability of the brokerage industry. Some brokerage firms were on shaky financial ground, and the possibility existed that customers would rush to withdraw their money and securities, thereby causing the firms to fail. To head off the possibility of a run, the government and the industry promoted an organization that would provide financial security for customers of the brokerage industry in the same way that the Federal Deposit Insurance Corporation (FDIC) provides financial security to the depositors of commercial banks.

SIPC insurance is designed to protect customers of a failed brokerage firm when the firm's assets are insufficient to satisfy customer claims. The insurance does not reimburse investors for losses in a stock's market value that result from stock market fluctuations. Investors with financial claims that exceed SIPC's coverage become general creditors of the failed firm. There is some concern among industry professionals that the failure of a major brokerage firm would result in substantial delays in SIPC reimbursements to the firm's customers.

Some brokerage firms provide for protection of the assets in customer accounts by purchasing private insurance in addition to the insurance provided by the SIPC. Brokerage firms sometimes provide this additional insurance only for certain types of accounts. For example, asset management accounts offered by several of the large brokerage firms nearly always include additional account insurance.

CHAPTER 5

Techniques for Investing in Common Stocks

Before deciding to buy common stocks or any other investments, you should determine what you expect your investments to accomplish. The financial goals that you establish will help determine the most effective investment techniques and the types of stocks to purchase. Most investors choose common stocks based on economic fundamentals such as expected earnings, inflation, interest rates, and so forth, although some investors are influenced mainly by technical analysis. Individual investors should seriously consider acquiring mutual funds rather than individual issues of common stocks.

By now you understand what common stocks represent, how stocks are issued and traded, and how to go about opening a brokerage account so that you can invest in these securities. You must still determine how much of your financial resources should be invested in common stocks and choose which stocks to buy. Buying common stocks without first having a clear idea of what it is you are attempting to accomplish, other than to become as rich as possible as quickly as possible, is likely to cause you to make faulty investment decisions in terms of the stocks you buy and the amounts you invest.

The Importance of Establishing Investment Goals

The first order of business in any investment program is to determine why you are investing. There must be some reason, or perhaps several reasons, why you have decided to set aside a portion of your current income. After all, investing requires that you give up a portion of your current income that could otherwise be used for new clothes, a weekend at the beach, or any of the many other things you would like to own or do. Presumably you are investing in order to attain some particular goal or set of goals that you have judged to be important. You may have in mind a long-term goal such as accumulating an adequate retirement fund, or you may be saving to accomplish an intermediate-term goal such as putting together enough money for a down payment on a home. You should also consider establishing short-term goals such as a pool of liquid investments that is available for emergencies and for making annual property tax and insurance premium payments.

Avoid purchasing the common stock of a company with a story that is so complicated you find it impossible to understand. If you don't know why you want to buy a stock, you should avoid it regardless of the enthusiasm of the person who is recommending that you part with your money. Complicated stories are for stocks that can't be recommended on their basic merits.

The financial goals that you establish are major factors in determining the kinds of investments you should acquire. Certain investments are better suited for meeting short-term goals, while others are more appropriate for meeting long-term goals. For example, a money market account at a financial institution is adequate for meeting short-term goals, but it is not the best choice for meeting long-term goals. If you feel that you need assistance to identify your goals and to determine how much money you need to put aside to meet these goals, you should acquire a copy of *The Guide to Personal Budgeting,* another book in the Globe Pequot Money Smarts series.

Unless you are interested in speculating on short-term price movements, common stocks are best suited to help you achieve long-term goals. Common-stock prices often vary substantially from day to day and from week to week, and it is risky to invest in these securities when you know that you will need to sell the stocks in a relatively short period of time. You may choose a stock that you expect to increase in value but then be required to sell the stock when the stock market has just suffered a particularly large decline. On the other hand, if you acquire common stock to meet a long-term goal, you have substantial flexibility in determining when to sell the stock. As a result, you can ride out temporary declines in the stock and in the market as a whole.

Investment Characteristics
of Common Stocks

Once you determine that common stocks possess the general characteristics you seek in an investment, the next step is to determine which stocks to purchase. Although common stocks all tend to share certain general investment characteristics, individual stock issues often have their own peculiar quirks. Some stocks are desirable for the dividend income they provide, even though they are likely to have limited prospects for increases in market value. Other stocks have a history of modest dividend payments but substantial increases in value. Some stocks tend to exhibit very modest price fluctuations, others very significant fluctuations. Many stocks offer stockholders the potential to earn very large returns, while other stocks have a limited potential for increasing in value.

It is always dangerous to try to predict the future when it comes to common stocks, but it is possible to categorize individual issues of common stocks in order to understand how the stocks are likely to perform in various economic climates. The values of certain stocks are strongly influenced by changes in interest rates, while those of other stocks are affected more by forecasts of economic activity or expectations regarding inflation. Several investment classifications, along with the characteristics of stocks falling into each of these classifications, are described below. Keep in mind that an individual stock can be included in more than a single category and that a stock can move to a different category when there are changes in a firm's financial structure, management, and business outlook.

Blue-Chip Stocks—Blue-chip stocks are the common stocks of companies that have a long and favorable history of earnings and dividends. A blue-chip company is likely to rely on debt to finance some of its assets but not to the degree that the debt is considered to endanger the company's future. Dividend payments on blue-chip stocks are secure and can generally be expected to increase steadily but gradually in future years. The market prices of blue-chip stocks are affected by movements in the overall stock market but to a lesser degree than the prices of most stocks. Blue chips can be expected to decline in value during periods of recession, but the underlying companies are likely to survive harsh economic periods while other, less strong companies will falter.

Blue-chip stocks are best suited to conservative investors, although most investors should have at least a portion of their funds invested in these securities. Blue-chip stocks represent stability and a relatively secure source of dividend income for investors, but the relatively long and distinguished history that characterizes these stocks means that the companies are mature and that there is less potential for large increases in value compared with stocks of younger, riskier companies. Blue-chip stocks include the common stocks of such well-known companies as American Telephone & Telegraph, Amoco, Coca-Cola, Eastman Kodak, Exxon, General Electric, Minnesota Mining and Manufacturing, and Procter & Gamble.

Cyclical Stocks—Cyclical stocks are the common stocks of companies with sales and profits that are strongly influ-

> Avoid the urge to sell a stock as soon as it has gone up a couple of points. It is just as difficult to watch a stock you have sold continue to rise as it is to watch a stock you own decline in price.

enced by general business activity. Cyclical companies make very large profits during periods of strong economic activity and make small profits or suffer losses during periods of economic weaknesses. The dividends of cyclical companies are likely to experience major changes that are in line with changes in income. Companies engaged in home building and in the manufacture of durable goods such as automobiles, steel, aluminum, and copper are examples of cyclical companies.

The stocks of cyclical companies experience relatively large price movements, although these movements are likely to precede changes in profits because stock prices generally lead changes in economic activity. For example, the stock of a cyclical company is likely to begin moving upward prior to the company's improving profit reports. Cyclical stocks can be part of any portfolio, although most investors will not want to invest a large proportion of their assets in these securities.

Defensive Stocks—Defensive stocks tend to hold their values during stock market declines. A defensive stock is likely to decline in price during an extended market decline, but to a smaller degree than the overall market. For example, a defensive stock might lose 5 percent of its market during a period when the overall stock market declines by 15 percent.

Defensive stocks include the stocks of companies that operate in industries with relatively stable revenues and profits. These companies produce and/or sell products or services that even in a weak economy continue to attract customers. Electric utilities, supermarkets, and retailers that sell staples tend to have stable revenues and income. The common stocks of American Electric Power and Winn-Dixie are examples of defensive stocks.

The downside of owning defensive stocks is that these securities tend to underperform the overall stock market during periods when the market is rising. During a period when the market rises 15 percent, a defensive stock may increase by 7 or 8 percent. Defensive stocks have less price volatility than the overall market, which makes them appropriate for conservative investors who are seeking stocks to meet intermediate-term goals such as purchasing a new car or taking an extensive vacation.

Growth Stocks—Growth stocks are the common stocks of companies that are consistently able to experience superior growth of revenues and earnings. Some companies experience growth that is a continuation of growth that has occurred over many years, while other companies are in the early stage of what promises to be an extended period of revenue and profit growth. Future rather than past growth classifies a business as a growth company, although many investors judge the future on the basis of past performance. Growth companies tend to retain a large portion of earnings to help pay for additional assets that will produce revenue growth in future years. High earnings retention means that growth companies pay relatively meager dividends.

The stocks of growth companies tend to sell at a relatively high price compared to current earnings (i.e., a high price-earnings ratio) because the stocks are priced on the basis of substantially higher future earnings rather than actual current earnings. One risk of owning a growth stock is that the actual growth of the firm's earnings could turn out to be considerably less than investors expect, and the stock price could thus decline to reflect a reassessment of the firm's future.

Growth stocks offer investors the potential to earn a relatively large return from increases in a stock's market price. At the same time, an investor who buys a growth stock risks the possibility of substantial losses in value if the firm's growth turns out to be less than anticipated. A major decline in the stock market will cause growth stocks to decline proportionately more than the overall market. During periods when the stock market is moving upward, growth stocks will frequently outperform the overall market. Growth stocks are especially appropriate for meeting long-term goals, but you should keep in mind that a stock that is considered a growth stock today may not be considered one ten years from now. Current growth stocks include Coca-Cola, Disney, Merck, Microsoft, Procter & Gamble, and Wal-Mart.

Income Stocks—An income stock pays a large dividend relative to the stock price. For example, at a time when most common stocks have a dividend yield (the annual dividend divided by the stock price) of 4 percent, an income stock may have a dividend yield of 8 or 9 percent. A high dividend yield generally identifies a company that pays a large proportion of its earnings in dividends. Investors are normally unwilling to pay a high price for a dollar of current earnings because the underlying companies have limited growth potential.

Income stocks are especially appropriate to include in

your portfolio if you are a conservative investor who wants to maintain a high current income. Income stocks exhibit relatively small price fluctuations because the stock prices are supported by generous dividends. This stability is an important and desirable characteristic when the overall stock market is experiencing weakness. Income stocks nearly always qualify as defensive stocks.

Speculative Stocks—Speculative stocks offer investors the possibility of very large gains at the risk of suffering very large losses. The stocks of companies that are heavily in debt, or that rely on a single product to produce all of their revenues, or that have the potential of winning or losing a major lawsuit, or that explore for oil, are all examples of speculative stocks. Growth stocks that sell at a very high price compared to earnings can also be considered as speculative stocks because these stocks often exhibit large price movements (both positive and negative).

Speculative stocks appeal primarily to investors who are willing to accept the possibility of substantial losses in return for the prospect of earning very high returns. Speculative stocks are popular with investors who buy and sell stocks in hope of earning quick gains. These common stocks also appeal to investors who believe they know of important factors relating to the stocks' values that have been overlooked by other investors. If you consider yourself to be a conservative investor, you should avoid investing much money in speculative stocks. If you are seeking to attain long-term goals and have a tolerance for some risk (i.e., not knowing the return you will earn), you can include speculative stocks in your overall portfolio, although it is a mistake to rely too heavily on these volatile securities.

Determining a
Common Stock's Intrinsic Value

Most investors make investment decisions based on the premise that each common stock has an intrinsic value—a "true" value that is based on all of the factors that are relevant to the stock. Although it may seem as if common stock should always sell at a price that represents its intrinsic value, stocks frequently sell for more or less than the facts warrant. The disparity between a stock's intrinsic value and its market value may result from the investment community not having access to all of the relevant facts. For example, a manufacturing company may be in the process of negotiating a major sale, something known only to a few members of management. Or, a small mining company may remain relatively unknown to all but a few investors.

Your task is to determine which stocks sell above their intrinsic values and which sell below their intrinsic values. Stocks that are priced below their intrinsic values are candidates for purchase. The problem is that a stock's intrinsic value is difficult to determine.

The task of estimating a stock's intrinsic value is known as *fundamental analysis*. It involves a study of economic forecasts, revenue projections, interest rates, management quality, a firm's indebtedness, national and world political

Beware of very low priced stocks. Common stocks that sell for $1, $2, or even $5 per share often entail substantial risk—more than most individual investors should assume. Stocks that sell for a low price nearly always do so for a reason: they aren't worth much.

climates, and a host of other variables that affect a company's value. Fundamental analysis is an ongoing exercise because the factors that influence a stock's intrinsic value are constantly changing. A financial analyst may judge the intrinsic value of General Motors' common stock to be $35 per share today only to change this estimate to $42 a month later, following an analysis of additional factors relating to the company.

Financial analysts spend many hours and consume substantial resources attempting to calculate the intrinsic values of common stocks. Unless you feel that you can do the job better than the professionals who devote a lifetime of experience to the task of identifying undervalued stocks, you will probably select common stocks on the recommendation of someone else. The recommendations may originate with your broker, from financial columns in newspapers, from comments made on a television program, or from investment advisory services that you subscribe to or read in your local library. You will probably benefit most by concentrating on determining what types of stocks are best suited to meet your goals and estimating how much money you should be investing in common stocks. As a novice investor you should rely on professional financial analysts who are experienced in judging the relative values of common stocks.

Using Technical Analysis to Select Common Stocks

Some investors select stocks to buy and sell on the basis of *technical analysis*. This is the examination and use of historical data to project future price movements of individual stocks and of the stock market. Technical analysis frequently takes the form of analyzing a price graph (the daily or weekly high price, low price, and closing price) for a particular stock. Investors who use technical analysis (called *technicians*) believe that a stock's past price movements are a clue to its future price movements. Over time, price movements plotted on a graph form familiar patterns that indicate whether a stock can be expected to rise or fall.

Other technical analysis includes the examination of stocks that are being actively traded to determine if there is excessive speculation. Technicians are also interested in the trading activities of small investors, who tend to make bad investment decisions. According to this rule, it is time for you to sell stocks when small investors are buying common stocks. Another technical rule concerns the actions of investment advisors: if an unusually large number of investment advisors are bullish (i.e., expect the market to rise), it is time to sell stocks. Conversely, if a large number of investment advisors are bearish (i.e., expect the market to drop), you should be buying stocks.

Dozens of stock-price formations and literally hundreds of other technical rules are used by technicians to decide which common stocks to buy and when to buy them. Technical indicators can also be used to determine when to sell common stocks. At least, this is the position of investors who believe that technical analysis is a useful way to make investment decisions.

Technicians' use of historical relationships stems from the belief that a cadre of informed and wealthy investors possess important information relative to common-stock values that is unavailable to the general public. Informed investors include investment groups that control large sums of money and that are able to gain insights concerning stock values that elude the majority of investors. An individual investor can make profitable investment decisions by determining what actions are being taken by informed investors and then following suit. If price charts and trading activity indicate that informed investors are accumulating shares of Apple Computer, for example, it is time for the individual investor to buy shares of this stock.

Some investors use a combination of fundamental analysis and technical analysis to construct a portfolio of common stocks. Fundamental analysis, or at least reliance on investment advice that is based on fundamental analysis, is used to select stocks that should be purchased. Technical analysis is used to determine the best time to purchase these stocks.

It is beyond the scope of this book to investigate fully the topic of technical analysis. So many investors use technical analysis to make investment decisions that any book about common stocks must include an introduction to this component of investment thinking.

Spacing Your Common-Stock Investments

If you are a conservative investor, it is generally a mistake to invest very large amounts of money in common stocks at any given time or during a short period of time. The stock market experiences wide price swings, and there is always a possibility that you will choose to invest a relatively large sum of money in common stocks at a time when the market is close to what will turn out to be the high point of a long cycle. Such an unfortunate decision is not unusual because investors often become excited about investing in common stocks only after reading and hearing about the large profits that are being earned by other investors. The stories and the profits tend to occur during the final stages of major bull markets. A more cautious approach is to make a series of investments over an extended period of time. A similar caution applies when you sell common stocks: beware of selling large amounts of stock at one time unless, of course, you need to liquidate a portion of your portfolio to raise cash for meeting one of the major goals you have established. Individuals sometimes become discouraged with the performance of their investments and dump their stocks when the market is near its lowest point. Some stock market analysts believe that the best time to invest in the market is when individual investors become so discouraged that they begin to liquidate their holdings of common stocks.

If you feel that you want to invest in common stocks but you are uncomfortable attempting to outguess the market, an investment technique called *dollar cost averaging* may offer a solution. It is an example of a formula investing plan that takes the decision of when to invest out of your hands.

Dollar cost averaging consists of investing a constant dollar amount of money in selected common stocks over a long period of time. You continue to invest the same dollar amount every month or every year no matter how the stocks perform and no matter how depressing the investment environment becomes. Dollar cost averaging assumes that investors are unable to judge the best time to invest and that the best policy is thus to invest the same amount of money each period, regardless of whether stock values are high or low or have been increasing or decreasing. Dollar cost averaging indicates the amounts you should invest and

Never buy stock over the telephone from someone you don't know. Do not be swayed by talk of great profits and "sure things." High-pressure sales operations employ salespersons who sell stocks just as they would sell used cars. Don't even stay on the line to listen to the whole pitch.

the timing of your investments so that you are required only to identify the stocks you intend to purchase.

Suppose you determine that you should be investing $3,000 each year in common stocks. At the end of the first year, you make the initial purchase—60 shares of a stock with a market price of $50 per share, for a total investment of $3,000. The following year, after the stock has declined in price to $40 per share, you purchase an additional 75 shares with your annual $3,000 investment. The greater the decline in the stock price, the more shares you will purchase with a constant investment. In the above example you will have invested $6,000 and acquired 135 shares for an average cost of $44.44 per share during the initial two years of your investment plan. Dollar cost averaging produces an average cost per share that is less than the average price at which the stock has sold.

The Importance of Diversifying Your Common-Stock Holdings

An important principle for putting together a sensible investment program is to invest in such as way that you achieve adequate diversification. You should choose investments that have different characteristics so that when some investments perform poorly, others will provide more favorable returns. The need for diversification applies to your overall investment portfolio, which is likely to include a home, a pension, and securities. You should also have a goal of diversification with respect to your investments in common stocks. You should not invest all of the money you allocate to common stocks in a single stock or in a small group of stocks that have similar investment characteristics.

Most investors who choose to invest in individual issues of common stocks find it impossible to achieve adequate diversification. Suppose you are able to invest $500 a month in common stocks. You may consider $500 to be a substantial sum of money, but such a small investment permits each stock purchase to consist of only a few shares and results in relatively high brokerage commissions. Investing such small amounts makes it impossible to achieve a diversified common-stock portfolio even after several years of investing.

Investing in Mutual Funds to Achieve Diversification

You can easily achieve diversification, even when investing relatively small sums of money, by choosing to invest in mutual funds. Mutual funds are investment companies that use investors' money to purchase securities. Rather than invest in inventories, equipment, and buildings, like manufacturing companies and many service companies, mutual funds invest in financial assets such as common stocks, corporate bonds, and U.S. government securities. The return you earn by investing in a mutual fund depends on the investment success of the fund's manager. If the manager makes good investment decisions and acquires securities that pay good dividends and interest and increase in value, the fund will prosper. If the manager of the mutual fund makes poor investment decisions, your investment in the fund will do poorly.

When you invest in shares of a mutual fund, you place your money in the hands of a professional portfolio manager. The fund will continually invest millions of dollars in many different securities that are chosen by the manager. Some mutual funds limit their investments to common stocks, while others invest only in bonds or a combination of stocks and bonds. Certain mutual funds invest only in U.S. government securities or in tax-exempt municipal bonds.

The manager of a common-stock mutual fund attempts to identify undervalued stocks in which to invest the fund's money. At the same time that new stocks are being purchased, the manager will continually evaluate stocks the fund already owns in an attempt to pinpoint overvalued stocks that should be sold. A manager may consider a stock to be overvalued because it has increased dramatically in price since the date of purchase or because there have been some negative developments relative to the underlying company.

A mutual fund's shares are valued on the basis of the total market value of all the securities the fund owns divided by the number of the fund's shares that are outstanding. The result is the fund's *net asset value* (NAV). Suppose a mutual fund currently owns three different issues of common stocks: 100 shares of a stock that sells at a price of $20, 200 shares of a stock that sells at a price of $25, and 150 shares of a stock that sells at a price of $40. The total market value of the mutual fund's holdings is $2,000 + $5,000 + $6,000, or $13,000. If a thousand shares of the mutual fund are out-

Stay away from stock options. A stock option gives an investor the right to buy or sell (depending upon the type of option selected) a particular stock at a predetermined price. These are complicated investments that can produce high returns and large losses. One thing that options do produce is a lot of commissions for your broker. Many investors have lost a great deal of money after becoming involved in options. Do yourself a favor and avoid them.

standing, the net asset value of the shares is $13,000/1,000 shares, or $13 per share. In practice, of course, mutual funds will own hundreds of different issues of common stocks.

A mutual fund's NAV is an important statistic to understand because it determines the price you will pay to purchase shares of the fund and the price you will receive if you sell your shares. Unlike the typical corporation, a mutual fund stands ready to redeem any outstanding shares that are owned by investors who wish to liquidate their holdings. In other words, rather than having to sell shares of a mutual fund to another investor as you would with common stock, you can sell them back to the mutual fund. Some mutual funds sell their shares directly to investors. Other funds distribute their shares through financial institutions such as retail brokerage firms.

Many mutual funds limit the types of common stocks they own. Some funds buy only the common stocks of companies engaged in a particular industry (these funds are called *sector funds*), while other funds specialize in the common stocks of companies that have a majority of their operations in a particular foreign country or in a particular region of the world. Actually, there are probably one or more funds that specialize in virtually any possible sector of the financial markets. If there are enough investors with the money and desire to invest in common stocks of a certain type, you can be certain that the mutual fund industry will offer a fund that meets the need. The danger of owning the shares of mutual funds with specialized portfolios is that substantially less diversification will subject you to a high degree of risk.

The Costs of Investing in Mutual Funds

Professional investment managers do not give away their time and expertise. If you choose to invest in a mutual fund, you will be required to pay an annual fee that is calculated as a percentage of the assets managed by the fund. Most mutual funds charge an annual management fee of between .5 percent and 1.25 percent of the assets managed by the fund. The management fee is deducted from the mutual fund's assets and results in a reduced return to the fund's shareholders. A mutual fund's management fee is designed to cover the expenses of operating the fund, including salaries and overhead.

Many mutual funds charge investors a sales fee, or *load*. A sales fee is levied to provide compensation for the sales-people who sell the fund's shares to investors. Sales fees typically range from 3 percent to 7 percent of the amounts that are invested in a fund. If you invest $5,000 in a mutual fund that charges a 5 percent sales fee, you will be charged $250, meaning that only $4,750 of your money will be used to purchase shares of the fund. Some funds charge a fee on re-demptions rather than on the sales of their shares. A sales or redemption fee is a one-time charge, unlike the management fee, which is levied annually. Mutual funds that do not charge a sales fee are called *no-load funds*. No-load funds are managed in the same way but sold in an entirely different way than mutual funds that charge a sales fee. No-load funds are sold directly to investors so that there is no salesperson to be compensated. Advertisements for no-load funds appear in numerous financial publications, including nearly every issue of *The Wall Street Journal*. The advertisements typically include a toll-free telephone number that investors can call to have questions answered or to obtain applications. Money to purchase shares can be mailed or wired to the fund.

You should invest in some reading matter regarding mutual funds prior to investing your money in one of them. You should have an understanding of how these funds are organized, how the value of mutual fund shares is determined, and how income earned by mutual funds is passed through and taxed to shareholders. With regard to an individual mutual fund, you should understand what types of stocks the fund purchases, how your shares can be redeemed, what charges are levied against the fund's owners, and how the fund's historical returns have compared to similar funds and to the overall market. It is very important to select a fund that has a stated investment goal that is compatible with your own financial goals. If you are young and are investing to attain long-term goals, you will probably be comfortable investing in a mutual fund that seeks to attain capital growth. If you are more conservative and have goals of an intermediate-term nature, you may want to invest in a mutual fund that seeks a combination of growth and income.

CHAPTER 6

Sources of Information about Common Stocks

A n investor must know where to obtain descriptive and statistical information that pertains to common stocks. Many sources of investment information are available at public libraries, college libraries, and brokerage companies, via radio and television, by mail, and via computer. To have the chance of being an informed investor, an individual must have access to information that pertains to the overall economy and to specific industries as well as information that concerns particular stocks.

Suppose you are reading the newspaper and come across an article about an exciting new drug that researchers feel will be effective in reversing certain types of arthritis. You are unfamiliar with the company mentioned in the article and would like to investigate the possibility of investing in the firm's common stock. Where can you locate information about the company? The company's stock may be unavailable because all of the shares are owned by a few individuals and the stock is not publicly traded. If the stock is publicly traded, the trading may occur on an organized exchange or on the over-the-counter market.

If you intend to invest in common stocks, from time to time you will want to be able to obtain various kinds of investment information. What is the price-earnings ratio of Occidental Petroleum common stock? What are the comparative earnings trends of several major computer companies? What are the five largest electric utilities? What was last year's rate of inflation? Does GTE have an outstanding issue of preferred stock in which you can invest? At one time or another you will have questions similar to these. The material in this chapter should help locate investment information.

Sources of Economic Information

Economic information includes data such as consumer prices, business activity, personal income, corporate profits, the unemployment rate, interest rates, government deficits, the balance of payments, and forecasts of economic output. Each of these economic variables can have an important impact on common stock values. Other than *Barron's*, the

Sources of Information about Common Stocks

> Keep informed about the stock market so that you don't have to rely on friends and co-workers to offer you secondhand and thirdhand information. Spend time each day reading the financial pages of your local newspaper.

sources noted below are publications of the U.S. government and can be found in library reference sections. Ask for a librarian who is familiar with reference materials.

Barron's is an inexpensive and widely available weekly newspaper that serves as a source of current economic and stock market data. *Barron's* is published each Monday by Dow Jones, the publisher of *The Wall Street Journal*. A large section at the back of each edition contains extensive statistics on interest rates, economic activity, monetary data, and a host of other economic variables, along with pages of data on the securities markets. The economic statistics in *Barron's* are current because it is a weekly publication. The paper is sold at many newsstands and is available at nearly any library.

Business Conditions Digest is published monthly by the Census Bureau of the U.S. Department of Commerce. This publication contains economic indicators, including the much-watched index of leading indicators, which provides guidance on future changes in economic activity. This publication is more likely to be found in a college library than a public library.

Economic Indicators is published monthly by the President's Council of Economic Advisors. It contains statistics on consumer prices, economic activity, employment, and government finance. It can be found in most college libraries and in larger public libraries.

Economic Report of the President is published each January to provide an overview of the economy during the past year and a look at the upcoming year. This excellent publication also contains extensive historical data on consumer prices, economic activity, and production.

The Federal Reserve Bulletin is the most widely available publication containing a large amount and variety of current economic data. This monthly publication of the governors of the Federal Reserve System is available in most public libraries. The *Bulletin* concentrates on statistics that relate to the banking system (e.g., reserves, deposits, loans, and so forth), but it also contains general economic information about economic activity, consumer prices, interest rates, and corporate profits, and a limited amount of stock and bond market statistics.

Monthly Labor Review is published monthly by the Bureau of Labor Statistics of the U.S. Department of Labor. The *Review* concentrates on articles and data relating to employment. Each issue contains data for the employment status of different population groups, unemployment by state, hourly earnings, wage rates, work stoppages, consumer prices, and producer prices.

Statistical Abstract of the United States is published annually by the Department of Commerce. This thick paperback is an excellent source of historical economic data (along with a whole host of other interesting statistics) on

Subscribe to *The Wall Street Journal*. *The Journal* is the daily bible of the financial markets, and you will learn an amazing amount about stocks if you spend at least a half hour each day reading this newspaper.

consumer prices, economic activity, interest rates, and so forth. The *Statistical Abstract* also serves as a reference for other information sources. The data are sometimes dated because it is an annual publication.

Survey of Current Business is published monthly by the U.S. Department of Commerce. The *Survey* is packed with approximately 150 pages of data on a wide variety of economic variables, including employment, corporate profits, dividend payments, retained earnings, business inventories, consumer prices, producer prices, industrial production, exports, cyclical indicators, and government finances. It is an excellent and up-to-date source of economic information that is available in nearly any library.

Sources of Industry Information

Suppose a friend recently told you that companies in the computer software business offer outstanding investment opportunities and you have decided to conduct your own research on the industry. You are interested in the industry's profitability, the rate at which revenues have been growing, and a professional view of the industry's outlook. Where can you find such information?

Many brokerage companies produce excellent industry research along with recommendations on the stocks of particular companies in an industry. Brokerage company research departments regularly generate reports on industries in which investors have an interest. Your task will be to locate a brokerage company that has a current report on the particular industry in which you are interested.

Forbes is a popular biweekly business magazine that publishes an "Annual Report on American Industry" in each year's initial issue. The survey includes industry overviews, along with limited statistics on individual companies within each industry. The reviews address the current condition of each industry and an analysis of what to expect.

Each spring and summer *Fortune* magazine publishes a series of special issues that contain listings and data on the 500 largest domestic firms in numerous industries. The initial and most widely used list comprises the 500 largest industrial companies (the frequently quoted "Fortune 500"). Subsequent issues contain lists for the 500 largest firms in retailing, financial services, utilities, and foreign companies, and even the second 500 largest industrials. Each May *Forbes* publishes a special issue that identifies the 500 companies with the largest sales, profits, assets, and stock market values. *Forbes* and *Fortune* can be found at most newsstands and in nearly every library. The January issue of *Forbes* and the *Fortune* issue containing the 500 largest industrial companies are good magazines to purchase and keep on hand for personal reference.

Standard & Poor's Industry Survey is an excellent publication that provides basic and current analysis of nearly seventy industries. The analysis includes a historical examination of each industry, along with S&P's view of the industry's outlook. This publication can be found in most college libraries, in larger public libraries, and at many brokerage company offices. Standard & Poor's is one of the country's largest publishers of business and financial information.

The Wall Street Transcript is an expensive weekly tabloid newspaper that provides some excellent industry analysis. Most issues spotlight a particular industry, with a roundtable discussion by financial analysts who regularly follow the industry's developments. Readers will also find reprints of brokerage-company research on specific industries. Each issue of the *Transcript* has an index for locating industry analysis that appears in the current issue. Cumulative indexes include entries in previous issues. *The Wall Street Transcript* is generally found only in relatively large libraries and at some brokerage firms. The amount of information in a single issue is nearly overwhelming.

Sources of General Stock Market Information

You may occasionally want answers to certain questions you have about the stock market. Which thirty stocks are included in the Dow Jones Industrial Average? How has the Standard & Poor's 500 Index performed during the past decade? What were yesterday's most active stocks on the New York Stock Exchange? There are several publications you can turn to for this type of general information.

AMEX Fact Book is published annually by the American Stock Exchange. This paperback book contains data related to events and market activity on the exchange during the year. The *Fact Book* can often be found in large libraries or can be purchased at a nominal charge from the American Stock Exchange.

Annual Report of the SEC (Securities and Exchange Commission) is an excellent source of historical market data and commentary on the state of the markets and on events of the year of the report. It can be found in the government documents' section of most large libraries. A drawback of this publication is the dated statistics that are inevitable in an annual publication.

Find out if a local college is offering a noncredit investments course. Such courses are generally inexpensive and allow you to ask questions in an informal setting. Beware of an instructor who has a vested interest in promoting a certain type of investment product.

NYSE Fact Book is a good source of current and historical data about trading activity on the New York Stock Exchange. One section of this paperback book is devoted to recapping events of the year, and another section contains extensive historical data on exchange activity. The annual price range of membership, current membership requirements, trading activity, and the most active stocks are all included. The *Fact Book* is published annually by the NYSE and can be found in some college libraries. It may also be purchased for a nominal charge from the New York Stock Exchange.

The Outlook is published weekly by Standard & Poor's Corporation and provides current information on the overall stock market and on specific industries and companies. This is an excellent and easy-to-read publication that will help you understand what is happening in the stock market. *The Outlook* is carried by most public libraries and by nearly all college libraries that offer a program in business administration.

The Wall Street Journal is an easily accessible source of up-to-date market data, including stock index movements and daily market activity. Each issue includes an analysis of the previous day's market activity on the exchanges and the over-the-counter market. Each issue of the *Journal* has an index on the second page of the second section. Libraries often maintain years of back issues of *The Wall Street Jour-*

nal on microfilm so that you will be able locate answers to such questions as "What were the most active common stocks on January 16, 1982?" and "What was the price of IBM common stock at the close of trading on February 15, 1987?" Many libraries subscribe to *The Wall Street Journal Index*, a must if you want to avoid spending days locating information about particular subjects or companies.

Barron's, the previously mentioned sister publication of *The Wall Street Journal*, contains a wide variety of weekly stock market data, including stock prices, trading volume, current earnings, and dividend information for NYSE, AMEX, and many OTC stocks. Dividend and earnings announcements during the previous week are highlighted in the statistical section.

Sources of Information about Particular Companies and Stocks

If you decide to invest in common stocks, you need to know where to locate information about particular stocks. Perhaps you were watching the evening financial news and saw a story about the improving prospects of a large West Coast bank. You wonder where you can obtain information about the company. Does it pay any dividends? What is the price-earnings ratio of the common stock? Is the stock traded on the New York Stock Exchange? There are a great many sources of information about individual companies and specific stocks, many of which are published by two large financial publishing concerns, Moody's Investor Service and Standard & Poor's Corporation. The following listing includes information sources that are relatively easy to locate.

Figure 14

HOW TO READ A COMMON STOCK LISTING

Major daily newspapers often carry three to four pages of stock price and volume data. The completeness of these listings varies with some papers carrying only the closing prices of selected stocks while other papers include substantial detail of the daily trading activity of each listed stock and most OTC National Market System stocks. A complete listing generally appears as:

52-Week									Net
Hi	Lo	Stock	Div	PE	Yld	Hi	Lo	Close	Chg
22½	14	Howell Tire	.90	8	4.5	20¼	20	20	+⅛

52-Week Hi & Lo—The highest price and lowest price at which the stock traded during the previous 52 weeks. Howell Tire stock has traded as high as $22.50 and as low as $14.00 per share during the previous year. You can compare the closing price with the annual high and low prices to determine if the stock is in an uptrend or a downtrend.

Div—The annual dividend per share. Howell Tire currently pays a dividend of $.90 per share annually. If you owned one hundred shares of Howell Tire, you would receive a dividend of $90 per year, or $22.50 per quarter.

PE—The price-earnings ratio calculated as the closing price of the stock divided by the firm's earnings per share. Howell's earnings per share are $20.00 divided by 8, or $2.50.

Yld—The dividend yield calculated by dividing the annual dividend by the closing price. This statistic does not include changes in stock price as part of the yield calculation.

Hi—The highest price at which the stock traded during the day.

Lo—The lowest price at which the stock traded during the day.

Close—The price at which the stock last traded during the day.

Net Chg—Net change, or the difference between the closing price and the closing price on the previous day. Howell Tire stock closed at $20.00, $.125 higher than the previous closing price. Thus, the previous day's closing price was $19.875.

Daily price quotations for stocks listed on the NYSE, the AMEX, and many entries on the OTC National Market System are published by *The Wall Street Journal, Investor's Daily,* and most large daily newspapers. Newspapers with smaller circulations may include prices for a limited list of stocks. More complete listings include data on dividends, the price-earnings ratio, daily trading volume, the daily price range, the closing price, and the change in price from the previous closing price. Newspapers with limited space may include only the closing price and change in price.

Brokerage firms that have research departments publish more reports on individual companies than you will have time to read even if you are retired. Unfortunately, you may encounter difficulty locating a current research report about a particular company when you need it. There may simply be no report available because there is little investor interest in the company. Even if you are able to locate a brokerage research report, you may find that the information is dated. The more brokerage companies you contact, the more likely you are to find the research you are seeking. If the brokerage company doesn't have a recent internal research report on a particular company, a broker is likely to provide you with a copy of a report from one of the commercial services noted below.

Annual reports are another source of corporate information. Although most annual reports are as much public relations tools (General Motors, for example, annually highlights the firm's new vehicle models) as they are reports on the firms' operations and financial status, the reports do contain a substantial amount of descriptive and financial information about what the firm does and where its revenues and profits originate. Many firms will send a free copy of their most recent annual report if you send a written request. Corporate addresses can be found in several of the publications listed below, including Moody's *Handbook of Common Stocks, Standard & Poor's Stock Reports,* and *The Value Line Investment Survey.*

A company with publicly traded securities files an annual Form 10-K report to the Securities and Exchange Commission. The report often contains information that is not included in the annual report to shareholders, although some firms make this special report a part of their annual report. Companies make Form 10-K reports available to shareholders and will often send copies to other individuals who request them. Some libraries subscribe to a service that provides Form 10-Ks on microfiche for 11,000 companies.

Companies that issue securities in a public offering are required to file a registration statement with the Securities and Exchange Commission. A prospectus is an edited and somewhat shortened version of the registration statement that may be obtained from the issuing firm or from one of the investment banks that underwrites the security issue. A prospectus contains information about what the firm does and what management intends to do with the money that is being raised from the stock issue. It also includes detailed financial data. Overall, a prospectus is a very good source of information about a particular firm.

Moody's *Handbook of Common Stocks* is a quarterly publication that contains a short analysis of and current and historical financial data for more than 900 widely held common stocks that are listed on the New York Stock Exchange and the American Stock Exchange. Moody's also publishes the companion *Handbook of OTC Stocks* for companies with stock traded on the over-the-counter market. Both handbooks contain current information on dividend dates and quarterly earnings, and an overview of each firm's financial structure (amount of debt and equity). Historical statistical information includes the range of a firm's stock price, earnings per share, shares outstanding, sales, debt, and several other important items. The publication has a listing of corporate officials and the firm's address and phone number. These publications are relatively inexpensive, and the *Handbook of Common Stocks* can be found in nearly every library and brokerage office.

Moody's Manuals are a series of large handbooks that are categorized by type of industry. Specialized volumes are published for transportation companies, banks and financial service firms, industrial companies, foreign corporations, and companies with stock that is traded on the over-the-counter market. The manuals, taken as a whole, contain a massive amount of information on more than 3,000 firms, including all companies with stocks listed on the NYSE and the AMEX. The manual includes abbreviated financial statements for seven years, a brief history of the firm, and a description of the firm's business. Fortunately, the entries are indexed so that locating information about a particular company is not a problem. These publications are expensive and can generally be found only in relatively large libraries.

Standard & Poor's Corporation Records is a series of large handbooks that contain information similar to that found in *Moody's Manuals*. Entries in the Standard & Poor's series are organized alphabetically rather than by industry. This service is expensive and can ordinarily be found in college libraries and large public libraries. Most college libraries carry either the *Moody's Manuals* or the *Standard & Poor's Corporation Records,* but not both.

Standard & Poor's Stock Reports is a quarterly service that consists of twelve paperback volumes: four volumes each for all companies with stocks listed on the NYSE, all companies with stocks listed on the AMEX, and nearly 2,000 companies with stock traded on the OTC market. Companies included in the service are listed in alphabetical order, and each listing includes two pages of historical information, including quarterly earnings, dividend dates, a graph of the stock price, and ten years of important financial statistics. Each listing also includes a summary of recent developments and a short-term earnings estimate. *Standard & Poor's Stock Reports* is carried by large college and public libraries. The information will be at least several months old, but this is a good source of information when you want a quick overview of a company.

The Value Line Investment Survey is an excellent source of investment information that is widely read and is carried by most libraries. The *Survey* is published weekly and consists of two parts. The smaller *Selection and Opinion* section contains an overview of the overall stock market, along with a recommendation and review of a stock that the firm's analysts feel is a particularly attractive purchase. The second and larger section of the *Survey* consists of one-page reviews of nearly 1,700 companies. The companies are organized by industry in thirteen separate editions. Each company is re-

Take time to become acquainted with the investments material in the reference section of your local library. If you are unsure what material is available or where to look, ask the librarian.

viewed once per quarter. *The Value Line Investment Survey* is somewhat different from the other services noted in this section because Value Line includes projections for financial data (earnings, revenues, dividends, and so forth) and makes a recommendation on the timeliness of owning the stock. The relative riskiness and timeliness of owning each stock is ranked on a one-to-five scale. An index to companies covered by the service is updated weekly.

OTC Special Situations Service is published by Value Line twice a month. Each issue contains information on a recommended stock, along with a summary of previously recommended stocks. This service covers only stocks traded on the over-the-counter market.

Investor's Daily is a daily newspaper that competes with *The Wall Street Journal*. The paper's listings include earnings per share and a relative strength ranking for each stock listed on the New York Stock Exchange and the American Stock Exchange and for stocks included in the NASDAQ National Market System.

Sources of Information
on Mutual Funds

Price quotations for mutual fund shares are provided on a daily basis by *The Wall Street Journal*, *Investor's Daily*, and many large daily newspapers. Complete listings include each fund's net asset value, offering price, and net price change. Most newspapers are unwilling to devote the considerable space necessary to include complete information on all mutual funds and instead carry abbreviated price quotations for a condensed list of funds. *Barron's* provides more detailed information on a weekly basis that includes performance data for each fund.

Forbes magazine publishes an annual survey of mutual funds each August. The survey categorizes mutual funds by the types of investments they hold (stock funds, foreign stock funds, bond funds, foreign bond funds, municipal bond funds, money market funds, and so forth), and grades each fund from A to F on the basis of the fund's performance in bull markets and bear markets. The special issue includes historical data on each fund's short-term and long-term investment performance and on the sales fee and the annual expense ratio. Addresses and phone numbers are provided for each of the funds or family of funds. *Business Week* and *Money* publish special issues with similar data.

Investment Companies is an annual publication of Arthur Wiesenberger Services that includes comprehensive reports on more than 600 mutual funds. Each report includes a brief history of the fund along with a sketch of the fund's investment philosophy, special services, fees, and investment performance. If there is a bible of mutual fund investors, this is it. Wiesenberger Services publishes a quarterly companion, *Management Results,* which provides more frequent updates of investment performance. *Current Performance and Dividend Record* by the same firm is a monthly publication that contains performance and dividend information for more than 400 mutual funds.

United Mutual Fund Selector is a biweekly publication of United Business Service Company. This publication includes articles on particular funds and performance comparisons among funds.

Sources of Computerized Data

Several firms provide computerized information that is of interest to common stock investors who own a personal computer. Some sources are on-line and must be accessed via long-distance telephone line by your computer's modem. Other sources are accessed via compact disks or floppy disks that are inserted in your computer's disk drive. Accessing data via a modem entails an access charge to the system and, for users who do not live in a large city, a long-distance telephone charge. Having financial and stock market data available on compact or floppy disk requires that you purchase the disks.

On-line databases include the *Dow Jones News/Retrieval, Compuserve, Dialog,* and *The Source.* These databases provide access to a huge amount of data, including current and historical stock prices, earnings forecasts, statistics from corporate financial statements, and articles on business and economic activity.

Computer disks with security prices and financial data are available from several sources. Financial data rapidly become dated, so a computer user who chooses the disk option must view this source of information as an ongoing commitment. On-line services provide databases that are constantly updated and thus are generally more current than data via disks.

Stockpak II by Standard & Poor's Corporation includes a database of up to 4,600 firms, depending on the level of service an investor chooses. The data include a wide range of financial statistics, including income, dividends, sales, and debt. A user of *Stockpak II* can establish a number of criteria and have the program scan the database to determine which stocks meet the established standards. For example, you might want the program to list the stocks of firms that have dividend growth of at least 5 percent, sales growth of at least 8 percent, and a debt ratio of no more than 20 percent. You can establish whatever standards you deem appropriate.

Compustat is a comprehensive service that is available on compact disk. Data include ten years of quarterly financial data and twenty years of annual financial data on approximately 10,000 companies. The data can be screened in a similar manner as explained for *Stockpak II*.

Value Line offers *Value/Screen Plus* on floppy disks. It includes stock prices and financial data for nearly 1,700 companies that are regularly covered by the *Value Line Investment Survey*. The program allows an investor to screen the data in the same manner as explained for *Stockpak II*.

CHAPTER 7

The Risks
of Owning
Common Stocks

Investing in common stocks entails several risks that can prove quite costly to an investor. Dividends that are paid to stockholders may not keep pace with inflation or may be reduced or even eliminated. Stock prices are subject to substantial variations that make it difficult for a stockholder to know how much will be received when shares of stock are sold. Stockholders of a company with bad management or too much debt may find that their investment loses most or all of its market value. Careful selection of stocks can keep risk within acceptable limits.

Investment risk is caused by uncertainty concerning the rate of return that you will earn from an investment or a group of investments. The less certain you are of the return you will earn, the greater the risk of owning an investment. The risk is especially great when there is a possibility that a large negative return (i.e., a substantial loss) can result. Some investments, such as certificates of deposit and U.S. Treasury bills, are considered to be virtually risk-free because the owner of such investments is certain of how much money will be received and when the receipt will occur. Both items are promised by the borrower and included in the agreement. In addition, both are guaranteed by the U.S. government or a U.S. government agency. Most other investments entail at least some degree of risk. For example, a corporate bond subjects investors to the risk that the corporation that issued the bond may be unable to meet its financial obligations.

Common stocks can be very risky investments to own. Nearly all common stocks subject investors to substantial uncertainty regarding the rate of return that will be earned. Stock prices are extremely volatile, and it is not unusual for the market price of a common stock to move upward or downward by 20 percent or more during a year. A stock that sells for $50 per share in January may reach a high price of $65 and a low price of $35 before the end of the year.

Income from common stocks is uncertain because, unlike interest payments to bondholders, dividend payments to stockholders are not a legal obligation of the company. Dividends must be approved by a company's board of directors, which may decide to reduce or even eliminate the payments if the firm encounters financial difficulties. At the opposite extreme, the directors of a successful company may not raise the dividend as much as you expect. Dividends are much easier to estimate accurately in the near term than the long term because it is difficult to forecast the business conditions a firm will face many years in the future.

Figure 15

1991 PRICE RANGE FOR SELECTED STOCKS

Stock	12/31/90 Price	High Price	Low Price	12/31/91 Price
American Tel & Tel	$30⅛	$40⅜	$29	$39⅛
Bally Manufacturing	2⅛	6½	1⅞	5¼
BellSouth	54¾	55	45⅜	51¾
Cooper Tire & Rubber	17⅛	52¾	15¾	51
Detroit Edison	28¼	35⅜	27¾	34¾
Exxon	51¾	61⅞	49⅝	60⅞
Horizon Health	1⅝	11¼	1⅝	10⅜
James River	26¼	29¼	17	20
Kimberly Clark	87⅛	104½	76	101⅜
Nevada Power	21⅞	22½	16⅝	19⅜
On Line Software	6¼	15¾	5⅛	15¾
Readers Digest	29½	49	26⅛	48⅜
TCBY Enterprises	5¾	9¼	9¼	5¼
Wal-Mart	30¼	59⅞	28	58⅞

Risk of Loss Caused
by Unexpected Inflation

Brokers often tout common stock as an investment that is a hedge against inflation. The hedge stems from the fact that shares of common stock represent ownership in a business that owns assets that should increase in market value during periods of inflation. The market values of office buildings, factories, land, and machinery should be positively affected by inflation—that is, the greater the amount of inflation that occurs, the more these assets should increase in value. If a period of inflation results in an increase in the market values of assets owned by the business, the value of the business itself should increase, thereby causing shares of ownership in the business to increase in market price.

An increase in the market value of assets during a period of inflation stems partly from the higher cost of reproducing the assets. Inflation is accompanied by higher labor and material costs, which makes buildings more expensive to build and equipment more expensive to manufacture. Increasing asset values also result from the positive effect that rising prices can have on a company's profits. Businesses sometimes view a period of general inflation as a cover for increasing their own prices for the goods and services they sell. Customers are less likely to complain about price increases for a product during a period when most goods and services are increasing in price. If customers complain, the business blames the increased prices on higher costs that must be passed along. Increased prices should translate into increased profits for the company and increased dividends for the company's stockholders. Thus, stockholders are pro-

> Beware of buying a common stock just because it offers an unusually high dividend yield. A very high dividend yield is often an indication that investors don't believe the company's dividend will be maintained at the current level.

tected against inflation by increasing asset values and by increasing profits and dividends. At least this is the theory.

In practice, inflation affects different types of companies in different ways. Unexpected inflation is usually accompanied by rising interest rates, increased labor costs, rising materials costs, increased transportation costs, and higher plant and land costs. Businesses with mostly fixed costs that can easily raise prices to their customers are likely to prosper during periods of inflation. A company that incurs these increased costs but that is unable to increase the prices of its own products or services will have its profits squeezed, sometimes to the point that they turn into losses. Reduced profits are likely to translate into a lower price for the firm's common stock, thus subjecting stockholders to the double whammy of owning a stock that is falling in price during a period of rising consumer prices.

As a common stockholder you will lose purchasing power unless the stock price and dividend payments increase enough to offset rising consumer prices. If a company is able to increase its profits and dividends by 5 percent annually during a period of 9 percent annual inflation, stockholders of the firm will experience a decrease in the real purchasing power of the dividend payments they receive. Stockholders will experience even greater losses in purchasing power if inflation causes profits and dividends to decline.

Risk of Loss Caused
by Rising Interest Rates

Rising interest rates can result in lower returns on common stock for two reasons. Reason number one is that increasing interest rates cause an increase in interest expense for businesses that rely on short-term loans to finance a portion of their assets. Many businesses have outstanding loans with interest rates that automatically change whenever market rates of interest fluctuate. Loans with variable interest rates cause a business to incur higher interest expenses when short-term interest rates increase and to experience lower interest expenses when short-term interest rates decrease. Higher interest expenses will have the effect of reducing a company's profits, which may affect the dividends the business pays to its common stockholders.

Higher interest rates also cause a business to encounter increased interest rates on new loans that are taken out by the business. The higher interest expense on new loans will have the effect of reducing profits compared to the profits that would be earned if new loans could be made at the previous, lower, rate of interest. The negative effects of new loans at higher interest rates can have a large impact on the profits of expanding companies that need to raise a lot of money to pay for additional assets. Rising interest rates also affect the profits of companies with outstanding loans that must be refinanced. For example, a company may have a $10 million loan that will soon come due and must be refinanced at whatever interest rate is in effect at the time of the refinancing. If the existing loan has an interest rate of 7 percent and the refinanced loan will have an interest rate of 10 percent, the company will have additional annual interest expenses of $300,000.

Reason number two is that higher rates of interest have a negative effect on nearly all investment values, including stock prices, as discussed in Chapter 2. Reduced stock values result from stocks being required to compete for investors' money with alternative investment vehicles. If interest rates rise, causing certificates of deposit and bonds to offer higher yields, common stocks will decrease in market price until the stocks offer investors an expected return that is competitive with that of bonds and CDs. The more market rates of interest increase, the more common stock prices must fall in order to offer yields that investors deem adequate.

Risk of Loss Caused
by a Poor Business Environment

The value of a business and the market price of the firm's stock are influenced by the ability of the business to earn a profit for the firm's owners. A downturn in a company's revenues and profits will probably cause investors to decide that shares of the company's stock are less desirable to own, thereby causing the shares to decline in price. When a company's revenues are subject to large and unexpected variations, there will be great investor uncertainty concerning the profits the company will earn and the rate of return that the firm's common stockholders will earn.

Wide swings in revenues are a major cause of business risk, especially for businesses that have large fixed operating

> Common stocks traded on the over-the-counter market are generally riskier to own than those listed on the New York Stock Exchange and the American Stock Exchange. OTC stocks also tend to offer the potential of higher rates of return than stocks listed on the exchanges.

costs. Fixed operating costs include expenses such as salaries, depreciation, and overhead, which cannot be easily changed, at least in the short run. Airlines routinely face changes in ticket prices and passenger traffic that cause large fluctuations in revenues. At the same time that airlines have volatile revenues, they also operate with very high fixed costs that continue regardless of the amount of revenues earned. The bottom line is that airlines are subject to a high degree of business risk that translates into substantial risk for investors who own airline stocks. Business risk is also relatively large for the stockholders of cyclical companies such as auto manufacturers, steel manufacturers, home builders, and appliance manufacturers.

Some types of businesses are less affected by uncertain business conditions. Stockholders of firms with stable revenues are subject to less risk of reductions in dividends or share prices because of deteriorating business conditions. For example, retail supermarkets tend to be affected less than most companies by swings in business activity because people spend about the same amount of money on groceries regardless of changes in business conditions. A business recession may actually cause individuals to purchase more groceries as they attempt to save money by eating out less often. Likewise, electric utilities generally experience relatively small and fairly predictable swings in revenues. Stockholders of businesses that operate in either of these industries are subject to less risk from swings in business activity than are stockholders of most other businesses.

Business risk is also caused by the possibility that management will make decisions that will result in losses to a firm's stockholders. A company's chief executive may decide to invest in a new, untried manufacturing technology that turns out to be flawed and unworkable. Or a firm's loose management structure may result in division managers making decisions that are incompatible with the company's overall plan, thus causing the firm to lose direction and the stockholders to suffer reduced values for their shares. Some chief executives and corporate boards do a poor job of planning for management succession, especially when the same individual has been at the helm for many years. Having someone who is an unknown quantity assume the reins of a company with a long history of rising profits can cause substantial uncertainty on the part of investors.

Risk of Loss Caused by a Company Being Heavily in Debt

Companies that choose to finance a large proportion of their assets with borrowed money face an increased possibility of being unable to meet their financial obligations. The greater a company's reliance on debt, the more likely it is that the company will be unable to service the resulting interest and principal payments. A large amount of debt also tends to produce large variations in a firm's earnings, which places the stockholder in a riskier position because it is more difficult to forecast earnings and dividends.

A company that relies mostly on the firm's earnings and

on owner contributions to pay for new assets has few fixed financial expenses to meet. A company with few fixed financial expenses is apt to be able meet its financial obligations when it encounters difficult economic conditions. A business with a lot of debt can encounter trouble when revenues decrease or increase more slowly than the firm's management expected at the time the funds were borrowed.

If being in debt is so risky, why do most companies employ this method of financing? The answer is that debt allows a company to acquire more assets and grow more rapidly than would reliance solely on earnings and stockholders' contributions. A company that conscientiously avoids borrowing money may have to delay its expansion plans because of the limited amount of funds available to pay for new assets. Delayed expansion may allow the firm's competitors to gain an advantage by being the first to reach new markets or develop new products.

Another potential advantage of borrowing is that debt financing will earn a higher return on the stockholders' investment when the company experiences favorable business conditions. A decision to seek a long-term loan at a fixed rate of interest can prove to be very profitable if a company's productivity and revenues grow. The fixed interest expense means that a greater proportion of revenue growth is likely to be left for the stockholders.

Risk of Loss Caused by Market Fluctuations

Nearly every type of investment other than those of a very short-term nature, such as savings accounts and money market funds, experiences fluctuating market values. House prices increase and decrease from year to year and during different seasons of the same year. Likewise, market prices are constantly changing for collectibles, gold, commodities, and long-term corporate bonds. Common stocks are no exception. They often sustain price increases and declines for no particular reason and in an unpredictable manner. Common-stock prices routinely bob up and down even when there are no changes in expectations regarding market rates of interest, inflation, or earnings.

Unpredictable changes in stock values are not an important risk for investors who have long investment horizons. If you are investing in common stocks in order to provide for a retirement that is not expected to begin for several decades, there is little reason to be concerned that the prices of your stocks fluctuate. On the other hand, if there is a possibility that you will need to liquidate a portion of your investments on relatively short notice, variations in the market values of common stocks are an important risk because you may find yourself needing to sell shares of stock when prices are at a temporary low.

Certain stocks exhibit large price fluctuations, while others tend to have stable prices. You can gain insight into a stock's price stability by looking at historical price data. Most stocks that have exhibited large price fluctuations during the past several years are likely to continue to do so. Likewise, if a stock has been trading in a relatively narrow price range, you can generally count on a continuation of this price stability. If you may have to liquidate a common stock on relatively short notice, you should consider relative price fluctuations to be an important consideration when you select stocks.

Risk of Loss Caused
by Infrequent Trading

Investment assets that are seldom traded may be difficult to sell unless you are willing to offer a price concession to attract a buyer. It is especially difficult to obtain a fair price when you are in a hurry to sell an asset that has little trading activity. Many stocks are actively traded and offer good liquidity to a seller, even when it is necessary to sell the stocks immediately. At the opposite end of the liquidity scale, some stocks in which limited trading occurs may be difficult to sell on short notice unless you are willing to accept a price that is lower than would be received in an active market.

The ownership of inactive stocks is not a great concern if you are investing for the long term. The common stocks of relatively small, little-known companies frequently offer an opportunity to earn large capital gains. Unfortunately, the infrequent trading caused by a current lack of investor interest means that you may have difficulty disposing of the stock at a reasonable price on very short notice. If you are investing to achieve short- or intermediate-term goals and expect that you will have to sell your stocks in the not-too-distant future, owning stocks that don't have an active secondary market is a risky investment choice. You can avoid

Build up an adequate emergency fund before you begin investing in common stocks. Every person and family should have ready access to a pool of money. Common stocks are not good investments for funding an emergency fund.

this risk by limiting your selections to stocks that are actively traded. If liquidity is important, you should choose stocks that are traded on one of the organized exchanges or that are among the more active stocks on the OTC National Market System.

Judging the Risk of Owning a Stock

There are several methods by which you can gauge the risk of owning a particular common stock. Brokerage companies often include an evaluation of risk when they produce a research report on a common stock. A report might indicate that a stock is for speculative accounts only, or there may be a relative risk assessment based on an established scale. Some investment advisory services also address the issue of risk. For example, the *Value Line Investment Survey* includes an assessment of risk for each stock that is evaluated by the service. Risk is judged on a scale of 1 to 5, with a ranking of 5 being reserved for stocks that are judged to be among the most risky.

Financial theory has produced another measure of risk for common stocks that is now widely used by both individual investors and portfolio managers. *Beta* is a measure of the degree to which changes in a stock's return are affected by changes in the return of the market. Stocks with a high beta tend to be strongly affected by stock market changes, while stocks with a low beta tend to be less affected. The beta of the market and of the average stock is 1. Betas of .8 and less are generally considered to be low, while betas of 1.2 and above are considered to be high. Stocks with a beta of 1.2 and above are relatively risky to own although they also offer the potential to earn a high rate of return.

There are several sources of common stock betas. Some brokerage companies calculate and publish betas for selected stocks. *The Value Line Investment Survey* includes betas for each of the stocks that is evaluated by the service. Keep in mind that beta is a measure of the degree to which a stock is affected by market movements and not a measure of the total risk of owning a particular stock. Also keep in mind that some analysts believe beta is a poor measure of risk because there is some evidence that a stock's beta can change over time.

In addition to market risk, common stockholders also face uncertain returns because of the risks that are unique to a particular company or a particular industry. Unique risks, also called *nonmarket risks,* include such uncertainties as an airline's rising cost of jet fuel, the possibility of disease or an infestation of pine beetles for wood products companies, possible labor strife for automobile companies, and the possible failure of a newly developed drug to achieve FDA approval for a drug company. These uncertainties are very important to companies that operate in industries that are affected by the uncertainties. They are less important to companies that operate in other industries and to the overall economy.

Your total risk as an investor in common stocks is a combination of market risk and nonmarket risk. You can reduce but not eliminate market risk by investing in stocks with low betas. You can eliminate nonmarket risk as a major concern by carefully constructing a diversified portfolio of stocks. A diversified portfolio of common stocks that have low betas is a low-risk portfolio.

The Risk of Owning
a Portfolio of Stocks

It may seem as if the risk of owning a group of stocks must be approximately equal to the average of the risks for each of the stocks that is included in the group. According to this theory, if you own a portfolio that is comprised of two stocks, and each of the stocks is subject to large price fluctuations, the returns of the two-stock portfolio will also be subject to large fluctuations. In truth, fluctuations in the returns on your portfolio are likely to be smaller—perhaps considerably smaller—than the fluctuations in the returns on each of the stocks.

Fluctuations in the returns on your portfolio depend both on the fluctuations in the returns of the individual stocks you own and on the degree to which the fluctuations in the stocks are correlated. If the returns on the two stocks fluctuate in a similar manner (i.e., the returns on the stocks increase and decrease together), then fluctuations in the returns on the portfolio will mirror the fluctuations in the returns on each of the stocks. If the fluctuations in the returns of each stock are not related, then fluctuations in the returns on the portfolio will be reduced. If the fluctuations in the returns on each stock are negatively correlated (i.e., when the return on one stock fluctuates upward, the return on the second stock will fluctuate downward), the fluctuations in returns on the portfolio are likely to be quite low. A carefully constructed portfolio of stocks can subject an investor to a level of risk that is much lower than the average of the risks associated with each of the stocks considered individually.

The uncertainties that are unique to a specific company

> Don't invest too much of your savings in common stocks. There should be a place in your portfolio for other kinds of investments, including a money market account, bonds, and tangible assets.

are less significant when you own a portfolio that includes ten or twelve different stocks. A sudden increase in the price of petroleum will result in a substantial rise in the cost of jet fuel and will reduce the profits of airline companies. The industry's increased expenses and reduced profits are likely to affect the return you earn from owning an airline stock. The increased cost of petroleum products will have less effect on companies engaged in other businesses and on the rates of return you earn from owning the stocks of these other businesses. If your portfolio includes the common stock of a petroleum company, for example, the reduced return you earn on the airline stock may be offset by an increased return on the petroleum stock. Such are the wonders of diversification!

The Importance of Diversification

A traditional method for reducing the risk of owning common stocks is to acquire stocks that have a diversity of investment characteristics. If most of your portfolio is comprised of the stocks of companies in a similar line of business, you will find that an event that affects one stock is likely to affect the other stocks in the portfolio in a similar manner. Not only do you not want all your eggs in one basket, you want to make certain that the baskets are in different locations (i.e., that the stocks are in different industries) in case some unfortunate event affects one of the eggs. Acquiring a group of stocks with similar characteristics defeats the purpose of having a portfolio—the reduction of risk. Your goal should be to construct a portfolio that is comprised of stocks that are influenced by different events.

Proper diversification means that your selection of a stock should be influenced by the effect the stock will have on the risk of your existing portfolio. If your portfolio already includes a substantial amount of utility stocks, you should consider placing additional investments in other kinds of businesses even though you may consider utility stocks to be a particularly good buy. Likewise, if you are heavily invested in the stocks of natural resource companies (i.e., mining, petroleum, timber, and so forth) you should consider investing additional capital in other types of industries.

The investment goals you have established are another important ingredient in determining the stocks that should be included in your portfolio. If your investment goals are primarily long term in nature, you should build a stock portfolio that is aimed at meeting these long-term goals. If your main investment goal is to have a stable source of income, you should own stocks that pay liberal dividends. Keep in mind that constructing a portfolio of stocks that meets your investment goals does not lessen the need to maintain a diversified portfolio.

Glossary

Ask The price at which a security is offered for sale.

Bear market An extended period of declining stock prices.

Bid The price offered for a security.

Blue chip An investment of very high quality.

Book value per share The amount of stockholder investment in a company measured on a per share basis.

Broker A firm or person who brings together a buyer and a seller. A broker facilitates a transaction but does not actually take possession of the asset being transferred.

Broker-dealer A firm that acts as a broker and also as a dealer. Many large brokerage companies are broker-dealers.

Bull market An extended period of rising stock prices.

Buy-and-hold strategy An investment strategy in which stocks are purchased and held for long periods of time rather than turned over rapidly.

Capital gain The margin by which the proceeds from the sale of a security exceed the cost basis.

Capital gains distribution The distribution of capital gains by an investment company to its stockholders.

Capital gains tax The tax levied on gains resulting from the sale of securities.

Capital loss The margin by which the cost basis of a security exceeds the proceeds from the sale of the security.

Cash account A type of brokerage account that requires an investor to pay in full for securities purchases.

Chart A graph displaying a stock's price and trading volume over a period of time.

Closed-end investment company A company that issues a fixed number of shares of stock and pools investors' money into a portfolio of securities.

Commission The fee charged by a broker to buy or sell a security.

Glossary

Common stock fund A mutual fund that restricts its investments to common stocks.

Contrarian An investor who makes decisions by going against the crowd.

Dealer A firm or person that purchases securities for its own portfolio and sells securities from this same portfolio.

Director A member of a firm's governing board.

Discount brokerage firm A brokerage firm that offers discounted commissions on securities transactions. Most discount brokerage firms do not offer investment advice to customers.

Diversification Acquiring a pool of assets whose returns are not directly related.

Dividend A portion of a company's profits that is paid to its shareholders. Most publicly traded corporations pay quarterly dividends.

Dividend reinvestment plan A plan that allows a company's stockholders to have their dividends automatically reinvested in more shares of the firm's stock.

Dollar-cost averaging Investing equal amounts of money at regular intervals.

Dow Jones Industrial Average An average stock price that is calculated daily by using the stock prices of 30 large industrial corporations.

Earnings per share Net income of a company divided by the number of outstanding shares of common stock. Earnings per share is an important influence on a company's stock price and dividend policy.

Exchange A facility in which securities are traded.

Ex-dividend A stock that no longer carries the right to receive the next dividend payment.

Fundamental analysis An evaluation of security prices based on established standards such as asset values, earnings, management quality, and economic factors.

Fully valued A stock that sells at a price that fully reflects the stock's fundamental value.

Going public Selling publicly all or part of a private company's ownership.

Growth stock A common stock that is expected to produce relatively large gains in value.

Glossary

Income stock A common stock that pays a relatively high annual dividend in comparison to the stock price.

Initial public offering (IPO) The first public sale of a company's common stock.

Investment banker A firm that helps businesses raise capital.

Investment company A company that pools investors' funds into a managed portfolio of securities.

Issue 1. To sell securities in the primary market. 2. A particular group of securities.

Joint account A brokerage account in the names of two or more individuals.

Limit order An order to buy or sell a security at a specified minimum price.

Listed stock A stock that is traded on an organized securities exchange.

Load The sales fee charged by a mutual fund.

Margin account A brokerage account that permits an investor to buy securities using borrowed money. An investor may also borrow money against securities that are held in the account.

Market order An order to buy or sell a stock at the best price available at the time the order reaches the market maker.

Most-active stocks Stocks with very high trading volume.

Mutual fund An investment company that continuously sells new shares and redeems outstanding shares of its own stock. Mutual funds pool investors' funds into an actively-managed portfolio of securities.

Net change The amount by which a security price has changed since its closing transaction in the previous trading session.

New issue A security being offered to the public for the first time.

New York Stock Exchange The largest organized securities exchange in the United States.

No-load fund A mutual fund that is distributed without a sales fee.

Odd lot Less than 100 shares of stock.

Over-the-counter market (OTC) A large network of dealers who are market makers in a wide variety of securities.

Payment date The date on which a dividend is paid to stockholders.

Glossary

Payout ratio The proportion of income a firm pays in dividends.

Preemptive right The right of a stockholder to maintain a constant percentage of a company's stock by being given the first opportunity to buy any new shares that are offered in a public sale.

Price-earnings ratio (PE) The market price of a company's stock compared to the company's earnings per share.

Primary market The market in which securities are issued by organizations raising capital.

Prospectus A document with financial and descriptive information relative to a new securities issue.

Public offering The sale of securities to the public.

Record date The date on which an investor must be listed as an owner of a company's securities in order to qualify for a dividend, annual report, or proxy.

Round lot One hundred shares of common stock.

Secondary market The market in which outstanding securities are traded among investors. The New York Stock Exchange is part of the secondary market.

Securities and Exchange Commission (SEC) The federal agency that is in charge of administering securities laws.

Securities Investor Protection Corporation The government-sponsored organization that insures customer accounts at brokerage companies.

Settlement date The date on which payment for a purchase or securities that have been sold must be delivered at a brokerage company.

Short sale The sale of borrowed stock.

Split An increase in a firm's outstanding shares of stock without a corresponding increase in the firm's assets.

Standard & Poor's 500 Stock Index A popular index that is used to measure movements of the stock market.

Stock dividend A dividend paid in additional shares of stock rather than in cash.

Volume The amount of trading that takes place in the market or in a particular security.

Index